W9-CAE-359

DATE DUE

SNOB ZONES

SNOB ZONES

Fear, Prejudice, and Real Estate

LISA PREVOST

Beacon Press
Boston

BEACON PRESS
25 Beacon Street
Boston, Massachusetts 02108-2892
www.beacon.org

Beacon Press books
are published under the auspices of
the Unitarian Universalist Association of Congregations.

16 15 14 13   8 7 6 5 4 3 2 1

A version of chapter 2 appeared as the article "What's So Bad About a Cottage?"
in the March 22, 2009, edition of the *Boston Globe Magazine*.

This book is printed on acid-free paper that meets the uncoated paper
ANSI/NISO specifications for permanence as revised in 1992.

Text design and composition by Kim Arney

Library of Congress Cataloging-in-Publication Data

Prevost, Lisa.
    Snob zones : fear, prejudice, and real estate / Lisa Prevost.
       pages   cm
    Includes bibliographical references and index.
    ISBN 978-0-8070-0157-8 (alk. paper)
    1. Zoning, Exclusionary—New England. 2. NIMBY syndrome—New England.
    3. Discrimination in housing—New England. 4. Housing development—New
    England. 5. Community development—New England. I. Title.
    HT169.9.E82P74 2013
    307.0974—dc23
                                                        2012041718

CONTENTS

T HIS BOOK BEGAN WITH a startling display of rude behavior. It was 2005, and I was covering a zoning hearing in Darien, Connecticut, an outwardly refined suburb known for its preppy, members-only mentality. This was a public hearing, meaning that the public was invited to come and complain about the development proposal under consideration. Rare is the human anywhere who shows up for one of these hours-long, weeknight meetings because they wish to compliment the developer. The citizens who do turn out are usually the handful of neighbors who live within view of the building site. But on this particular fall evening, the project in question was objectionable enough to have drawn a crowd of nearly three hundred.

Businessmen fresh off the train, older women settled in with laps full of knitting or magazines, serious-faced young couples in hushed conversation—the chairs in the Town Hall auditorium were nearly full by the time I arrived. I had an inkling of how the evening was going to go before I even stepped through the door. As I walked across the dark parking lot, a man a few steps behind me greeted a local television cameraman like this: "I can't believe you're here. Why don't you fucking shoot something else?"

The developers received a similarly warm reception. Throughout their presentation, the audience loudly snickered and hissed. Now, this might not have been so surprising in some northern backwater or a scrappy blue-collar burb. But this was Darien, and this wasn't just some average audience. This audience was made up of people who live in one of the most highly educated, exceedingly affluent communities in the country. These were people who had presumably learned their manners early on and refined them over time at one of the eight members-only clubs in town. And yet, here they were, receiving a scolding from the commission chairman for their discourteous and disruptive behavior.

What was it that not only brought out such a large crowd this evening but also brought out the worst in them? What made them feel so threatened? The news article I wrote immediately after that hearing came to a succinct conclusion: Darien residents were furious about a proposal to drop some affordable housing for seniors into an expensive neighborhood of single-family homes.[1] This was the obvious and overarching reason for their ire. File it under the subject line "NIMBYism" and call it a day.* Only this: the reaction that night seemed so out of proportion to the project at hand— twenty condominiums, six of them reserved for moderate-income seniors—that writing it off as simple NIMBYism felt disingenuous. Were people really this incensed because, as they had said, traffic might increase or because emergency vehicles might have a hard time getting in and out of the housing complex?

In the years since that night, I have delved much more deeply into the circumstances surrounding this conflict and numerous others like it in towns rich and not-so-rich.

I have waded into the hysteria surrounding a proposal for high-density cottage housing in a bedroom community more comfortable with five-thousand-square-foot colonials.

---

*NIMBY is the acronym for "not in my back yard." It is typically used to refer to kneejerk opposition to new development from nearby residents.

I have picked through the past of a quiet lake town that, despite its "live free or die" leanings, put a blanket ban on construction of multifamily housing.

I have searched for the dividing line between principled opposition and prejudice in a fishing village nearly torn in two by a modest proposal for six subsidized apartments for agricultural workers.

I have overstayed my welcome in a summer resort community where moneyed interests use their control of shore properties to keep fishermen and beachgoers at bay.

These clashes, laid out here by location, were not hard to find. Nor are they anomalies. These sorts of dramas play out with such regularity in what real estate agents refer to as "desirable" communities that the term "NIMBYism" has become a cliché. In fact, the very frequency of these battles, as well as the predictability of opponents' arguments, speaks to the assumed entitlement that is the subject of this book. It is a reflection of the widespread belief among homeowners that they have the right to restrict access to "their" community and limit other people's property rights for their own benefit. What gives them this power? The local authority to write zoning laws for their town.

In the broadest sense, zoning authority is a useful planning tool for safely and efficiently separating land uses for the good of the community. It prevents a slaughterhouse from opening up shop next to a school. It keeps developers from jamming in houses on every available vacant lot. But there is a point at which controls on growth and development cross the line to unnecessary, purely self-interested exclusion. And what I found in town after town is that many homeowners are more than willing to cross that line—and feel fully justified in doing so. They move to a place because they like the neighborhood or the schools, and then they expect that it will never change. They choose a place for the "people like us" factor, a place where they can feel comfortable that their kids will grow up around kids of the same class. They find a place that is still relatively undeveloped and figure this, at last, will be their escape from the complexities and compromises of more populous places. They come with all these expectations, and then when development challenges those expectations, as it inevitably will, they go straight to the local zoning code to point out that "we don't allow for this type of thing."

These were the words of a woman in the sparsely populated lake town I visited where a small affordable-housing complex was proposed for the village center. This woman said that before she'd moved to town, she'd checked out the zoning and was reassured to see that it did not allow for construction of any type of multifamily housing. This, she decided, was a place she wanted to be. Here was a place where the zoning was, in her words, "strict."

"Strict" is the polite term for what she was talking about. Strict zoning is prohibitive zoning, or what is less politely known as "snob zoning." This is zoning that blocks or sharply limits development of multifamily housing—subsidized housing, market-rate apartments, duplexes—and, in some cases, any residence that doesn't claim at least an acre of land. It is zoning designed to keep things a *certain way* for *certain people*. Homeowners in these towns tend to view multifamily housing proposals as an attack on the sanctity of local control—hence, the overwrought scene in Darien's town hall. Homeowners have conflated the right to *regulate* land uses for the public good with the right to *exclude*—not just uses, but people.

This is preservation of self-interest, plain and simple, a predictable human response. But in breaking down the arguments of the most vocal development opponents, the ones who typically draw the most attention and gain the most traction, I often found that what they considered threats to their self-interest were nothing more than figments of their irrational fears, misconceptions, and, yes, outright prejudice. This was particularly true when the project at hand involved affordable housing. Even though the workforce housing of today bears no resemblance to the public housing high-rises of the past—the poster child being Chicago's notoriously crime-ridden Cabrini-Green—local opposition is still one of the greatest impediments to its construction. Certainly some projects are more worthy of support than others, but towns would be a lot better off if they dedicated even half the time and money they spend on fighting affordable-housing developers to figuring out ways to create such housing on their own terms. "Like it or not, we're in a sad state of affairs," Bob Engler, a veteran affordable-housing consultant in Massachusetts, told me. "It took us a hundred years to get from the end of the Civil War to the Civil Rights Act. [We have] forty years of history in affordable housing, and we're still arguing about the same things."[2]

Snob zoning caters to the impulse to wall ourselves off in "safe" spaces. And as income inequality has widened across the United States, the impacts of snob zoning have become more stark, such that in many areas, town lines all but double as class lines.[3] The phenomenon only exacerbates deepening social inequities—the American credo of "opportunity for all" becomes a joke, after all, in towns where the zoning laws scream, "We were here first!" Decades of one-size-fits-all zoning and hostility toward afford-able housing have gradually squeezed out people of even average incomes from the most prosperous areas, areas with the most employment potential and the highest-performing schools.

These mean constraints on housing development are also a drag on future economic growth.[4] *Snob Zones* focuses on slow-growth, aging New England, where the cumulative consequences of inflexible zoning are particularly acute: loss of young people, suburban sprawl, concentrated urban poverty, costly highway congestion. The region's excessive aversion to housing density is also considered a major contributor to its steep housing costs relative to areas of the country with fewer constrictions on development. Those constraints on supply saved New England from the glut of vacant homes that dragged down states like Florida and Nevada during the housing crash, but that doesn't mean the region isn't still paying a price.

The widely held notion that the housing bust resolved the affordability crisis that has plagued New England and other high-cost areas like California and the metropolises surrounding Washington, DC, and New York City is a fallacy.[5] The bust did not compensate for the short supply of cheaper housing options in these areas, and, in fact, the accompanying recession and spike in unemployment further upped the demand, as hordes of Americans were forced out of their homes and into the rental market. Nationally, one in four renters now forks over more than *half* of his income just to cover rent and utilities. (Generally speaking, spending any more than a third of your income on housing is considered burdensome.)[6]

Home prices in New England have certainly deflated, but in four out of six of the region's states (the exceptions being Maine and New Hampshire), the reduction isn't enough to make the median-priced home reasonably affordable for the median-income household.[7] And in areas where jobs are most plentiful, rentals don't provide much relief. Demand is so high in Greater Boston relative to supply, for example, that the average rent reached an all-time record high of $1,665 in 2011.[8] When it comes to truly affordable rentals—those that are subsidized in some way to keep rents below the market rate—the supply runs so far short of need that when a new development opened last year in the shoreline community of Old Saybrook, Connecticut, more than two hundred families requested applications for one of sixteen townhomes.[9]

This book aims to reframe the usual narrowly focused debates around housing by casting the "we don't allow for this type of thing" crowd in a broader context and by showing how the "every town for itself" mentality ultimately works against the region's interests. The chapters on Darien and Roxbury, Connecticut, draw in part on my reporting for the real estate section of the *New York Times*. The chapter on Easton, Massachusetts, is loosely based on an article I wrote for the *Boston Globe Magazine*. The chapter on Watch Hill, Rhode Island, also began with a story I wrote for the *Times*, but compared to the rest of the book, it ventures farther afield to examine how moneyed interests are increasingly controlling access to the shoreline (a topic that deserves a book of its own). I included it here because I view it as an interesting branch of the "family" of conflicts over local control.

New England, as the original incubator for civil society and democratic values in the United States, proved a particularly poignant arena in which to explore the use and abuse of local control. Though each of these stories chronicles events in a particular place, they are not meant to demonize individual towns. Rather, they are windows on ways of thinking common to many communities, thinking that isn't always spoken out loud.

ONE

Rural Character for the Rich: Roxbury, Connecticut

B ARELY TWO HOURS FROM Manhattan in Connecticut's Litchfield hills, the town of Roxbury is notable for what it lacks.
Among the southernmost of the refined weekend warrens that
have come to define bucolic Litchfield County, Roxbury is well
within reach of the metropolitan sprawl that unceasingly laps from
below. And yet, it is manifestly untouched.

The boutiques, boarding schools, and galleries that draw visitors to many nearby towns are not to be found here. Save for a single small market, a subtle showroom for antiques, and one sit-down
restaurant called Mamies, Roxbury (pop. 2,200) has no shops, no
entertainment venues, no liquor store, and no inn. Office buildings
and medical facilities do not mar its scenic lanes. Municipal sewer
and public water are unavailable. So are sidewalks. And Roxbury
has not a single apartment house or condominium.

These absences create various complications for Roxbury residents—for example, having to move away when it's time to sell the
family house and downsize. But here, such inconveniences are upheld as virtues. As a member of the zoning commission once told
me, "We don't even have a traffic light. We're pretty proud of that."[1]

1

Residents even objected when the owner of the lone grocery market painted lines in the parking lot and designated handicapped spaces. Any "improvement" is eyed warily as a potential precursor of ruin.[2]

Yes, residents often have to leave town once they reach a certain age, acknowledges Peter Hurlbut, the town clerk and a descendant of Roxbury's oldest farming family. (He is the fourth generation of Hurlbuts to hold the town clerk's post, a bit of nepotism happily embraced here as tradition.) "I like to think people see it as a tradeoff," Hurlbut says. "Why would they move here otherwise?" Inconvenience is part of Roxbury's price of admission.

The province of dairy farmers big and small throughout the first half of the twentieth century, Roxbury now relies on a surviving Hurlbut farm, called Maple Bank, along with the holdings of several gentlemen farmers to authenticate its rural appearance. The most revered of the latter is Dudley Diebold, who holds together Toplands Farm, a 650-acre spread anchored by a barnyard with a blue silo atop a stunning outpost on Painter Hill. An heir to the Sterling Drug fortune, who found as a young man that he hated New York City, Diebold, now in his seventies, has lived on Toplands Farm much of his life. A going dairy operation until 1995, the farm's workings have long since dwindled to hay and firewood. Family subsidies have kept the acreage intact—or, as Diebold says, "We just keep pouring money into it."

Toplands is, in essence, a microcosm of Roxbury as a whole: impossibly pastoral, and handsomely underwritten to remain so. Located amid rolling hills in the Shepaug River Valley, Roxbury boasts more acres of open space than it has people.* Roadways twist and wind up steep hills that unexpectedly flatten to reveal broad views of open fields and the vast hills beyond. Pavement is not a given—dirt roads are considered chi-chi by the city dwellers

---

* As of 2010, the town had more than 3,600 acres of protected open space, most of it owned by the Roxbury Land Trust.

with second homes here. Homes constructed out of old barns are a common sight, more so perhaps than real barns. A ten-thousand-square-foot custom barn home set on the Shepaug River fetched $7.75 million in 2011; the lucky seller was Diego Arria, a former Venezuelan ambassador to the United Nations.[3]

Roxbury's whitewashed town center, with its tiny green, dueling church steeples, and smattering of municipal buildings, is a protected historic district. It is devoid of any commerce save for the market, which shares a building with a postage-stamp-sized post office and equally understated bank branch. "It's pretty neat that you can drive in at that green and know right what it was like fifty years ago," says Diebold.

A highbrow brood of writers, actors, and artists has availed itself of the opportunity to live in such splendid isolation ever since Arthur Miller settled into a Roxbury farmhouse and dashed off *Death of a Salesman* more than sixty years ago.[4] Seclusion came so easily in Roxbury that, at one point, Miller said that "spending more and more days of each week alone, I began to fear I was loving solitude and silence too much."[5] Nevertheless, Miller kept a residence in Roxbury right up until his death in 2005, when he drew his final breaths in the eighteenth-century farmhouse he'd purchased in the late 1950s with his then-wife, Marilyn Monroe. Other departed local luminaries include William Styron, Richard Widmark, and Frank McCourt, while current celebs include Dustin Hoffman, Denis Leary, Gay Talese, and Candace Bushnell. Their collective notoriety has in turn attracted the merely rich, many of them weekenders from New York, others full-time residents or nearly so.

Where the privileged part-timers find kinship with the many Roxbury residents of more meager-to-middling means (the dwindling core of natives like Hurlbut, retirees from away, telecommuting professionals) is in their fervent desire to keep the outside world at bay. They are naturally shielded to some degree, as the town's twenty-six square miles of hilly, rock-laden terrain don't easily lend themselves to dense development. And Roxbury's location well off I-84, the nearest interstate, tends to discourage commuters. But where natural obstacles to development leave off, strict land-use regulations begin. Houses must be built on very large pieces of land with at least 250 feet of frontage along a road. Space designated for commerce is minimal. Industry is prohibited. And the Roxbury Land Trust, with generous local support, has stockpiled some 20 percent of the town's total acreage for permanent preservation.

The end result is a far more beatific brand of rural than the Roxbury Arthur Miller fell in love with in the 1940s. In a paean written many years later, Miller recalled a roughhewn place peopled by a sour-smelling farm laborer who slept in a cinder-block cabin alongside his coonhound, an expert ox trainer with a basement full of hard cider, and the farmer whose parlor doubled as the town clerk's office.[6] Today, Roxbury's zoning regulations would likely preclude occupancy of a crude cinderblock structure, and most certainly would frown upon a high-traffic office in a residential area.

Sometimes, even the strictures of zoning can't block out development to residents' satisfaction. In such cases, they have proven most capable at manning the ramparts themselves. Nobody knows this better than Henrietta Rio R. MacKinnon Raikes.

AN AMBITIOUS YOUNG WOMAN of distinguished English ancestry, Raikes (who goes by the name Rio) moved to Roxbury in the 1970s while attending graduate school in New York. She lived on picturesque Painter Hill. The property actually belonged to her parents, she says, who'd asked her to find them something within driving distance of the city. Like so many others, Raikes chose Roxbury for its apparent quaintness. "It was a sleepy little backwater with one or two camera-shy people—William Styron, Arthur Miller—and very little in between," she recalls now. "It was like an

MGM childhood, you know? Sort of, prized cattle and little stone walls. I thought, how nice."

What transpired after Raikes moved in, however, was more reminiscent of a made-for-TV miniseries. Raikes shook the town awake when she revealed her plans to develop a small retail complex. Buoyed by her earlier success at renovating and selling a little house in town, Raikes partnered with a builder friend in the purchase of a six-acre parcel in the town's commercial zone, alongside the Shepaug River. This was the only area of town zoned for commercial use. "I thought, I will build something tiny and very attractive off the road," Raikes says. "I thought this was a good idea." The plan called for a larger market, as well as a hardware store, a barber, and a drug store. An architect friend helped with the design. And then, Raikes says, she stuffed copies of the plan in residents' mailboxes.

Almost immediately, Raikes learned where she'd gone terribly wrong. The commercial zone, it turned out, was a sham. Although it contained a business—an antique lumberyard—the zone was not really intended to invite any further activity. As town officials would later acknowledge, the commercial zone was deliberately put in an out-of-the-way location, and in a flood plain, on the assumption that no one would ever attempt to build there.[7] Another strong-willed young woman in town was determined to see that no one ever did.

This was Marianna Mayer, an author/illustrator who had been married to children's book illustrator Mercer Mayer. Mayer owned property along the river and had moved to Roxbury to escape the congestion of city life. She went head-to-head with Raikes, spearheading a citizens' group that circulated a petition calling for the elimination of commercial zoning altogether.[8] "The idea of there being a store in town was somehow offensive to these people," recalls Anthony Fitzgerald, one of Raikes's lawyers. "These were mostly people who stocked up on their groceries at Zabar's on their way out of the city. They didn't need a grocery market."

Not everyone in town felt this way, however, and the issue became bitterly divisive. "Town Split Open Over Shopping Center," read a headline in one local paper. Those aligned with Raikes were primarily locals who felt strongly about individual property rights or were simply tired of driving eight or nine miles every time they needed something. At a crowded public hearing on the proposal, "speaker after speaker stood up and said, 'We've got to preserve the rural character of our town,'" Fitzgerald says, "whereas actual rural characters were speaking about their desire for a store in town."

After weeks of furious feuding, Mayer's group won the first round. In one of the more scandalous moments in Roxbury history, the zoning commission pulled the rug out from under Raikes' project by simply eliminating the business zone, after the fact.[9] Raikes's request for a zoning permit was denied.

Calling the action "a dirty railroad job," Raikes and her business partner sued the zoning commission.[10] They also hauled the board before the state's Freedom of Information Commission for withholding minutes and other zoning documents from them. Testimony given in connection with the lawsuit revealed more questionable behavior: the board's secretary, William Hollingsworth, a real estate agent, had been quietly dating Marianna Mayer.[11]

Mayer (who still lives in Roxbury) insists that the relationship was purely platonic. But, in 1981, a state superior court judge cited the obvious conflict of interest as a factor in his finding that the commission's zoning switcheroo was both "arbitrary and illegal."

For Raikes, the ruling was a hollow victory. More than two years had passed since she had filed her application with the town. She was out of money, and the lending market had become far less friendly. "I'd lost about $120,000—legal fees, architecture fees," she says. "I didn't believe that public officials would stoop so low. I was just terribly naïve." She eventually left town and wound up in Italy's Tuscany region, where she ran her own exclusive medieval retreat.

Thirty years after that fiasco, Raikes's name is still occasionally heard about town. A few businesses do operate in the reinstated commercial zone—a daycare center, a café, the office of the builder who made barn homes fashionable. But the town's focus on "maintaining low density" and "preserving rural character" has not softened in the least, especially among those who moved to Roxbury for those charms. "People here are different," explains Marc Olivieri. A high-end builder in his fifties, Olivieri traverses between consultations with his wealthy clients and poker nights with his local pals. At both ends of the spectrum, he says, "they are reluctant to sell out for a gas station."

Roxbury's hyper-protective reflex is very good at serving the interests of individuals who wish to live apart from everyone else. The town's rich and famous frequently boast of their decision to pass over the crowded, egocentric Hamptons in favor of virtuous, small-town New England. As Anna Scott Carter, wife of *Vanity Fair* editor and Roxbury homeowner Graydon Carter, once told the *New York Observer,* "We rented a house in East Hampton for a couple of years and we loved it, but socially, there is too much pressure. For us, on the weekend, we want to get away and not see anyone."[12] This is somewhat disingenuous, in the sense that so many well-known New Yorkers are "hiding" together in the same towns—the Carters happen to be neighbors to Gay and Nan Talese in Roxbury center. Still, the second-home crowd is drawn by the rural New England look of the place, and, for Roxbury, the second-home crowd are the one and only industry.

On the other hand, the perfecting of the rural landscape has not been particularly conducive to maintaining a healthy human community. Increasingly, the only people who can afford to live in Roxbury are the very affluent, typically not the people who volunteer to rush into burning houses or sort through municipal-budget minutiae. "We've always had weekenders, but they've never been so wealthy and so removed," laments Georgette Miller over tea in the parlor of her antique colonial. Miller, who is active in historic preservation, moved to town in 1982. At that time, she says, "there wasn't this distance." She even recalls seeing Arthur Miller at town meetings.

The weakening of the community backbone is a sensitive issue in Roxbury. Not everyone is in agreement that maintaining its rural character must come at the expense of community. And the resentments this has spawned burst into public view a few years back, with the zoning commission once again at the center of the controversy. The contentious debate drew unwanted publicity. But it also begged a question that plagues high-priced towns throughout Connecticut's northwest corner: must the *look* of a community, insofar as it attracts high-end homeowners, take precedence over the community itself?

SINCE ZONING'S EARLIEST DAYS, the primary tool for "preserving rural character" in Litchfield County (as in many areas of New England) has been the mandating of large house lots. Large-lot zoning—that is, regulations requiring lot sizes of an acre or more for individual single-family homes—is a reliable method for keeping people out. This is partly a matter of simple math: A pie cut into four pieces feeds fewer people than the same pie cut into six pieces. The fortunate four merely receive big slices, and the remaining two are left without so much as a crumb.

In towns like Roxbury, without municipal water and sewer, the extra land around a house may (though not always) be needed to safely accommodate both a well and a septic system. Spreading out houses also reduces concentrations of stormwater runoff, which can harm water quality. Finally, placing houses far apart is aesthetically pleasing to those who prefer not to see their neighbors. Large-lot zoning, in short, works as a protective measure by limiting growth, safeguarding water supplies, and ensuring privacy. Those are its higher purposes.

But let's return to the pie metaphor. Say, once again, that the entire pie is cut into hefty slabs. No portion of the pie is sliced more thinly for those who require less. Not only does the pie then feed fewer people—it feeds fewer *types* of people. Only those people with big appetites and enough money may have pie. People who wish for only a sliver have two choices. They may either pay for a bigger slice than they need—provided they can afford to do so—or they can look elsewhere for someone willing to dish out a smaller portion.

This is how it is with towns, like Roxbury, that zone all or nearly all of their residential areas for single-family homes on large lots. People in need of smaller, less expensive properties—single people, young families, senior citizens, anyone closer to the mid-to-lower end of the income scale—are effectively invited to go elsewhere. And when whole swaths of a state are reserved for large lots—like much of Connecticut's northwest corner—people in need of more modest housing have to move farther away, or carry a heavy cost burden.

This exclusionary outcome was the original intent behind minimum lot sizes when they appeared as part of land-use regulations in the first half of the twentieth century. People moving from city to suburb were wary of being followed by the urban attributes they left behind.[13] So they willingly acquiesced to the expansion of local government power over land use (zoning) for the purpose of keeping out nuisances—namely, loud, polluting factories, bars, and saloons, as well as the poor, who were often immigrants.[14] Minimum lot sizes kept housing prices high enough to preserve class segregation and homogeneity.

A little more historical context is in order: Prior to the civil rights era, the US government actively encouraged zoning restrictions that preserved all-white, higher-income neighborhoods. The

Home Owners Loan Corporation—established under the New Deal to refinance problem mortgages—used a neighborhood appraisal system that devalued areas of mixed race/ethnicity or high density. The agency's highest ratings were reserved for new neighborhoods with homogeneous populations consisting of "American business and professional men."[15]

That bias also shaped the rapid, postwar suburbanization that followed World War II, when government guarantees made mortgages more widely available. The Federal Housing Administration, which insured the mortgages, viewed denser, more diverse neighborhoods as a greater risk. The reasoning, according to their underwriting manual, was that in order for a neighborhood to retain stability, "it is necessary that properties shall continue to be occupied by the same social and racial classes."[16]

After passage of the Fair Housing Act in 1968, civil rights activists turned their attention to the now firmly established pattern of housing segregation. The Suburban Action Institute, which was based in Westchester County, New York, attacked exclusionary zoning regulations as not just elitist but contrary to the free-market principles suburban residents claimed to hold so dear. In the words of cofounder Paul Davidoff, a planner and attorney, instead of allowing the housing market to freely respond to demand, suburban communities were using zoning to "protect their own very selfish desire to create a community that is amenable to themselves, but to prohibit the large mass of the population from sharing in those amenities. They have not bought the land, but instead have done the cheap and nasty thing of employing the police power to protect their own interest in the land and to exclude the largest part of the population."[17]

Since that time, various courts have reminded communities that their zoning power is not by divine right, but by state authority. As such, the courts have said, every community has a responsibility to consider interests broader than those inside their own borders.[18]

But these rulings do not prohibit the active use of large-lot zoning, and its exclusionary impact is no less real. A study reported in the *Connecticut Economy* found that a one-acre-higher minimum lot size reduces the "average" town's percentage of households with incomes below $50,000 by 5 percent. While that doesn't sound like much, the authors point out that since so many towns have minimum lot-size requirements and other restrictions, the collective effect on lower-income groups is much more substantial.[19]

Other research suggests that large-lot zoning also contributes to the high housing costs in much of the New England region by constricting supply. In the Greater Boston area, for example, the steady decline in building permits over the past twenty-five years is not due to a dwindling supply of land but to increasing constraints on construction. That was the conclusion of Harvard economist Edward Glaeser when he compared land-use regulations and building activity in 187 cities and towns in the Boston area. Communities with the largest supply of undeveloped land showed very low levels of housing construction. This, Glaeser argued, was the result of man-made land-use barriers. Large-lot requirements had the biggest stifling effect on construction between 1980 and 2002, with every extra acre per lot associated with 40 percent fewer building permits.[20]

Of course, today's advocates of large-lot zoning do not often go around talking about their desire to drive up prices and keep out the riff-raff. They talk about wanting to "preserve low density" and "protect rural character." But large-lot zoning should not be confused with protecting the environment. The environment would prefer that people take up far less space. Large-lot zoning does just the opposite and is therefore considered a major contributor to sprawl. A study by MIT's Center for Real Estate found that the average new single-family home built in eastern Massachusetts is consuming twice as much land as existing homes in those communities.[21]

"If you're serious about preserving open space then you *make* it open space," says Christopher S. Wood, a planner with Connecticut's Northwestern Regional Planning Collaborative. "People talk about large-lot zoning as a way of preventing residential sprawl. But say you have a five-acre lot with a house on it, and you also have a swing set, a tennis court, a barn, a garage, and a swimming pool. How is that not residential sprawl? The land still gets chewed up and cleared."

Yet large lots continue to dominate in the Northeast. As of 2008, the average minimum lot size in the region was one acre, more than twice the national average.[22]

IT WAS SUMMER 2007 when Roxbury's zoning commission alerted residents that the town's old nemesis, population growth, was banging at the gate. The timing of the pronouncement struck some residents as odd—even for Roxbury. Nobody in town had been publicly clamoring for a clampdown. Actually, housing development had slowed sharply since the 1990s. The year before, the town had issued just seven building permits for new homes, considerably fewer than the decade high of twenty-four.[23] It was true that the number of Roxbury residents had continued to climb—by about 200 people since 2000—but the actual *rate* of population growth was on the decline.[24]

Nevertheless, the zoning commission insisted that the town was under imminent threat. "We have a very attractive town here, obviously, because so many people would like to live here," Robert Falconer, then the commission's chairman, told a local reporter. "We don't want to be the fastest-growing town [in Litchfield County]."[25] Growth was changing the "rural character" of Roxbury, commission members said. And, so, it was time to raise minimum lot sizes again.

The majority of Roxbury was zoned for a minimum of three acres per house. (Smaller lots exist in the historic town center.) The commission proposed upping the minimum for most undeveloped property in town to four acres.

The skeptics scoffed. The wealthy people moving to town were buying up five, ten, twenty acres at a time. Upping the minimum lot size would have no relevance for these buyers. It might instead cause pain to those who could least afford it—older people with land they planned to subdivide and sell for retirement income, or younger people hoping to raise families in town. If anything, Roxbury needed some smaller lots, not larger ones.

One of the loudest critics of the growth-control plan was Robert Munson, the chairman of the town's planning commission. A burly general contractor, Munson oversaw a fairly powerless body that did little more than sign off on subdivisions. In Roxbury, zoners are appointed by the selectmen—the executive branch of small-town government—and write the regulations. Planners, who are elected, had been relegated to little more than a rubber stamp. But Munson still had a public megaphone, and he let it be known that, in his estimation, the zoners were reacting to a "growth" problem that didn't exist.

Munson grew up in Roxbury, back when his parents ran the lone market, and he'd witnessed both the piecing together of magnificent dairy operations like Toplands and Golden Harvest, as well as their slow demise. The most dramatic change in Roxbury, as for much of Litchfield County, had come in the 1980s, when the fever for conspicuous consumption helped spawn a new passion for second homes in the country. City dwellers looking to lay claim to pieces of agrarian authenticity swarmed Litchfield County, and the region's emerging identity as a more refined version of the Hamptons caused housing prices to soar. By the end of the decade, Roxbury's population swelled by nearly 25 percent.[26]

In response, Roxbury, along with many other towns in the area, tightened its zoning. The increased restrictions caused unease then, too, even among those who favored zoning protections. Peter Hurlbut's late uncle, Lewis Hurlbut, a farmer who was active in civic affairs, worried aloud that the growing rigidity around housing was forcing good people, both old and young, out of town. "Some of the outsiders would like fifteen-acre zoning to keep others out. That's a little too greedy," Hurlbut told an interviewer in an oral history of Roxbury. "We could pick an area in the town and set it aside, where young people can start out, perhaps with low-income housing."[27]

That didn't happen. A citizen-driven effort to develop housing for the elderly did go forward and was ultimately successful, but it took two decades. A local schoolteacher finally donated land for the development, Bernhardt Meadows, which has eighteen federally subsidized apartments.

Munson himself didn't want low-income housing in town. He viewed it as government meddling. But he thought the town had to do something to provide an opportunity for the creation of less-expensive housing. And so, though he accepted that rules on land use had prevented Roxbury from being overrun by development, he didn't see the need to sew the town up even more tightly. When the zoning commission began holding public hearings on its lot-size proposal, Munson spoke out, loudly. "What bothers me is that growing up in the town as a farming community, everybody looked out for each other, everybody mattered to each other," he told the *New York Times*. "Everybody got along, no matter what the class. Now, it's the individual that matters."[28]

The president of the town's volunteer fire department, Paul Elwell, also let it be known that he opposed the upzoning. Elwell was the local veterinarian; back in the 1970s, he had around eighty dairy clients in the area. Now he was down to fewer than ten, and it seemed to him that a share of community-mindedness had been lost with those farms.

Elwell hadn't grown up in town. But his father had. And Elwell had pored over photos from his grandfather's days, when Roxbury looked nothing like the carefully "preserved" place he now lived in. The Roxbury in the photos had smokestacks and industry and boarding houses and swaths of land cleared of trees. This was nineteenth-century Roxbury, when a boomtown briefly flourished around the riverside train station. An iron company employed some 150 workers at Mine Hill. Nearly as many worked in the busy granite, garnet, and mica quarries. Businesses sprang up around the busy station, forming a village known then as Chalybes.[29] The iron operation failed in the 1870s, and as the quarries too began to shut down, Chalybes gradually became a ghost town. Today, the old iron mine and furnace complex are part of a preserve, owned by the Roxbury Land Trust.

It amused Elwell when residents sermonized on the importance of keeping Roxbury "as it was." Those with a longer view might say Roxbury had never looked better! From his vantage point on the fire department, Roxbury was lacking in a vital resource: the people who keep rural towns running. So, at the same time zoners were looking to tighten the borders, Elwell stood before another group of Roxbury residents to make the opposite case. The occasion was a meeting on the town's long-term development plan, and the emphasis, as usual, was on conservation. Elwell suggested that the town could ease up on the housing restrictions a bit without sacrificing its rural ambiance.

"The last new member to join [the department] is over forty and that was within the last year," he told his audience. "We had four young members who moved out of town—they couldn't afford to live here. We need some hoof beats to replace us old goats. We don't have anyone coming along, and the same thing is true for the ambulance corps and most of the commissions in town hall.

"We are creating a Roxbury of people who are very willing to write checks," Elwell went on, "but those people are not the ones who respond to a fire in your house on a Saturday night."[30]

Looking back now, Elwell says he just wanted the town to make some room for housing that young people could afford. Doubters may argue that the periodic shortage of volunteers is more a reflection of busy schedules, but in Elwell's twenty-odd years with the department, he's found that people who want to volunteer make time for it, no matter how hectic their schedules. It's a matter of priorities. Perhaps more young people could live in town if officials allowed for—dare he say it?—condominiums. "Probably the Roxbury gods are about to unload on me for even using the word," he jokes. "But it doesn't have to be made out of brick and ten stories high with an airport light on top."

The *New York Times* editorial page made a similar suggestion when it weighed in on the minimum-acreage controversy. "Roxbury needs to be more creative," the editorial said. "The town runs the risk of being the exclusive enclave of well-to-do second-home owners and retirees fortunate enough to have bought property during a more affordable era. That is not a formula for a healthy or particularly diverse population."[31]

Since then, the 2010 US Census data has revealed that becoming an exclusive enclave wasn't just a risk for Roxbury. It was reality.

"THE TOWNS THAT PEOPLE knew twenty years ago are gone," says Dan McGuinness, executive director of the Northwestern Connecticut Council of Governments. "The age dynamics are totally different."

McGuinness was prepared for some of what he saw in the 2010 census data. He knew as well as anyone that the nine towns in the northwest region were having a tougher time recruiting volunteers from their aging and part-time populations. He'd jokingly commented on the changes himself in a 2007 report outlining the growing need for affordable housing: "The dearth of young families in some towns has become so pronounced that one local wag referred to his town as a place where old people go to visit their parents."[32]

But as McGuinness crunched the newly released census data, even he was sobered by the magnitude of the changes. The entire northwest corner looks lopsided. Northwestern towns have aged far more quickly than the state as a whole, partly as a result of a continuing influx of weekenders and retirees.

The graying phenomenon can be partly explained by broader demographic trends that are affecting much of New England. The population at large is aging as baby boomers begin to hit retirement, and, in Connecticut, the birth rate is one of the lowest in the nation.[33] Additionally, the state has lagged in job creation, which has caused some young adults to go elsewhere.[34] But the statewide demographic changes are magnified in the northwest corner—and glaringly so in Roxbury.

In a state with the dubious distinction of being among the oldest in the country, Roxbury is even older. Amid the perpetual fears about development bringing in too many expensive schoolchildren, Roxbury is looking alarmingly barren. And in spite of posting a 6 percent increase in total population over the last decade, Roxbury has rapidly shed young adults.

The most striking reversal is in the number of young children. The number of kids four and under in Roxbury declined by a dramatic 35 percent in the last decade, the largest such decline in Connecticut's northwest region. Enrollment at the Roxbury elementary school, the Booth Free School, has been slowly shrinking, but it is expected to plummet in coming years.[35] A school that educated 150 students in 2002 is projected to have closer to 70 in less than ten years. That could send Roxbury's per-pupil expenditure soaring, as fixed costs are divided among fewer students. As it is, as part of a regional school district spanning three towns, each with its own elementary school, Roxbury is already spending more than $20,000 per student.[36]

The sharp drop-off in young children makes sense given Roxbury's dearth of young adults. Roxbury residents between the ages of twenty-five and thirty-four are about 30 percent fewer in number now than in 2000. They represent just 6 percent of Roxbury's population, half the statewide average.[37] Residents aged thirty-five to forty-four are also down by a third. Meanwhile, the ranks of Roxbury residents between the ages of sixty and sixty-four have swelled by 97 percent (from 117 seniors to 231).

The median age in Roxbury is now fifty—a full ten years older than the median age for Connecticut as a whole.

The decline in numbers of young people coincides with the upward pressure on home prices prior to the market tumble. Prices are still so high that, as of 2010, Roxbury ranked sixth on a list of the least affordable communities in Connecticut.[38] With decent home-ownership opportunities under $400,000 still rare and affordable rentals limited to the occasional garage apartment, the town has a hard time even holding onto households that earn the median income for the northwest region, about $80,000.[39]

As the wealthiest town in Litchfield County, Roxbury can financially afford its pull-up-the-drawbridge mentality. The wealthy weekenders pay far more in taxes than they demand in services, thereby making up for the town's nearly nonexistent commercial base. The top ten taxpayers on the town's grand list are, in fact, homeowners. "That's our industry," says Gary Steinman, a biomedical engineer who operates a consulting practice out of his Roxbury home. "If we lost our rurality, we would lose that industry." But by refusing to make *any* room for higher-density housing, Roxbury is contributing to a regional affordable-housing shortage that affects most of the northwest corner.[40] What's more, as the census data shows, the price Roxbury pays for its "rural character" goes beyond dollars and cents. The toll extracted comes out of community.

MOST OF THE FORTY or so people who turned out for each of two public hearings on the four-acre proposal had nothing good to say about it. A local realtor, Wayne Piskura, said the change would unnecessarily reduce the number of lots a landowner could carve out of his property, which could cause financial harm to those with few other resources: "For some people, their land is their savings account, their retirement [fund]."[41]

Sarah Lauriat, a sixth-generation Roxburyite, read a letter from her father, John, who accused the commission of practicing "economic zoning." Rural character is not a matter of lot size, he said, but of interactions between townspeople.[42] Lauriat herself had managed to stay in town because her grandmother gave her Roxbury's most precious gift: land.

Among the commission members listening to the outcry was James Conway, a resident who also had deep roots in town. Conway managed what was left of Golden Harvest, now a pony farm called Thistledown owned by descendants of Frank Winfield Woolworth, founder of the F. W. Woolworth five-and-dime chain. Conway understood the concerns about the cost of housing in Roxbury, but he was nervous about easing up on zoning.

For Robert Falconer, the stern chairman (who, according to town land records, lived on less than four acres himself), the outcry was too little too late. The commission had been studying ways to control growth for two years, he said repeatedly. Residents had had plenty of time to weigh in on the issue before now. And he dismissed the charges of classism. "We don't have any hidden agendas—we're not excluding," he said. "We're trying to slow down the growth."[43]

In the spring of 2008, in a unanimous decision that assumed the support of a publicly silent majority, the zoning commission hiked Roxbury's minimum lot size from three acres to four.* Falconer closed the hearing by lauding his fellow commissioners for their noble act. "Some will not be happy," he said, "but I feel we have to act in the best interest of the town, and that's not always a popular position."[44]

LONG AFTER THE FOUR-ACRE question has been put to rest, Roxbury continues to tiptoe around the issue of creeping exclusivity. A few residents came together to study potential "smart growth" alternatives to large-lot housing. Joining them was a former resident, George Madsen, who lives one town over, in Woodbury. Madsen was born in Brooklyn, New York, but he considers Roxbury his hometown. When he was a boy, his family moved around a lot, and it wasn't until the age of thirty-nine, when he moved his own family to Roxbury, that Madsen felt truly at home. So he devoted plenty of time to giving back—including ten years as president of the Roxbury Land Trust.

But after twenty-seven years in Roxbury, Madsen and his wife reluctantly moved out. Approaching his seventies, Madsen wanted a smaller property requiring less maintenance, something that was unavailable in Roxbury. He found it at Woodbury Hills, a handsome condominium set back from the road with shingled, cape-style buildings around a center green with a white gazebo. The septic system for the development lay in an adjoining field. Condos started at around $275,000, not exactly cheap but accessible to the middle class.

Madsen sees no logical reason why Roxbury couldn't accommodate a similar development. "It just wouldn't have any impact

---

* The ordinance did try to prevent hardship on property owners who have just enough land to spin off one three-acre lot. It allows property owners with at least six acres to subdivide into two parcels of at least three acres each, if they meet other requirements.

on the sense of a rural community," he says. And though he hasn't lost his passion for environmental preservation, it is tempered by an appreciation for balance. "The more you preserve, and the more you keep the town pristine, the more it attracts the wealthy and becomes less affordable," he says. "We really should look at the thing holistically. What kind of a town do we want to be from a social aspect?"

There is sharp disagreement on the answer to that question. The "smart growth" group was interested in housing creation that would promote diversity, but "unfortunately," says one participant, Piskura, the real estate agent, "some people find that dangerous."

On a warm spring evening in 2010, Roxbury's zoning and planning commissions came together in a rare joint session to consider the "smart growth" group's suggestions. Affordable housing wasn't even contemplated. Even so, the report was not well received. "I don't want to come across as promoting this," cautioned James Conway, who was now the new zoning chairman. Such was the tone of the conversation throughout the night. People here were willing to *talk* about clustering homes or converting barns into apartments, but the conversation went in circles. Wouldn't such a change be risky? Could the land handle higher density? Would the townspeople stand for it? Would it cause taxes to soar? Was there even a market for smaller homes? And if so, were these would-be residents the kind of people Roxbury wanted? The people most likely to move into those smaller houses "are not all gonna be good guys from our hometown," Conway said. "There's some families that could move in from someplace that is not as pristine as Roxbury."*

---

* Asked later what he meant, Conway said he didn't mean to sound derogatory. Most everybody in Roxbury hires landscapers to take care of their yards, he said, and "people in smaller houses are trying to make ends meet, and might not have the time or money to keep up property the way Roxbury is used to."

Despite his misgivings, Conway would come back around to the discussion again and again in coming months, each time sounding as though he were trying to talk himself into the need for change as much as anyone else. Quietly nudging him along was the long-time first selectman, Barbara Henry. Popular with voters of every stripe, Henry had done the politic thing during the four-acre controversy by not taking sides. But it was she who appointed the smart-growth group, having come to believe there is a greater risk to doing nothing than trying something new. Older residents come to her when they're despairing over having to move away. She has watched solid folks leave, middle-class people who have given years to the town. And she doesn't like seeing the empty desks at the elementary school. "I absolutely believe we need to do something in this town," Henry says. "I don't want to be in a town where there are no children. I don't want to live in a gated community."

In the spring of 2012, zoning and planning were still kicking ideas back and forth. The possibility of converting existing homes and barns into apartments was off the table—renters and absentee landlords wouldn't take care of their housing, it was decided, and "a deteriorating housing stock" would "be contrary to the unique and rural traditional atmosphere Roxbury is known for."[45] The more suitable option was a subdivision regulation that encouraged smaller homes on smaller lots—maybe two acres each?[46] Discussion continued.

In the meantime, all residents had been invited to a special town-sponsored program aimed at planning for Roxbury's future. It was called: "A Town Conversation on Aging."

TWO

Dread of Density: Easton, Massachusetts

B EFORE THE HYSTERIA SET in, before the neighbors started with the trailer-park slurs and the lawn signs imploring passersby to "Save Our Neighborhood," and before one of them, a documentarian, began filming the whole affair, Charles "Nick" Mirrione tried to have a rational conversation with the people of Easton. A successful developer who got his start fixing up ratty multifamily rentals in the neighboring city of Brockton, Mirrione was used to opposition. He had encountered some level of resistance on nearly every residential project he'd undertaken in Easton. These ranged from clustered colonials on quiet cul-de-sacs to grand Victorians with custom weather vanes and boxy ranches restricted to the fifty-five-plus set. As in any fast-growing suburb—this one situated along the I-495 corridor about halfway between Boston and Providence, Rhode Island—once people moved in, they set about keeping others out. In Mirrione's thirty-five years in business, the arguments against new development had barely changed.

It all started in 2007, when the sky-high housing market had only begun to fall. Though he was still pursuing fifty-five-plus developments in other towns, Mirrione was also looking around for a new niche. He found that untapped opportunity in a rather glaring market incongruity. The newest houses in Easton had ballooned to an average of five-thousand square feet—double the size of homes built fifty years ago.[1] But as house sizes were swelling, household sizes were shrinking. Across the state—and the country, for that matter—households consisting of a single person or two people were now the majority, according to census data.[2] "I thought, 'Why are we building four-bedroom houses? Everyone's building four-bedroom houses,'" Mirrione says. So, he began thinking small. "I was sitting at my doctor's office, waiting, one day," he recalls, "and I was sketching a two-car garage with a little set of stairs going up to an apartment above. I was fooling around with it, trying to make it look cuter, like a barn." He was still fiddling with the concept when he came across an article with attractive photos of colorful little cottages in the Seattle area.

Only distant relations of the dark and drafty lakeside variety, these twenty-first-century cottages featured open floor plans, lots of natural light, and bright exterior colors. The design concept compressed the American ideals of suburban living into minia-turized form: domestic spaces downsized to less than a thousand square feet across two floors; the privacy of freestanding dwell-ings but closely clustered; individual patches of yard. The cottages were typically grouped around a central green to conserve land and promote community. It added up to an appealing formula that had people lining up to buy them. The biggest fans of cottage liv-ing turned out to be single, divorced, and widowed women, who represent nearly 60 percent of one-person households nationally.[3]

Intrigued, Mirrione flew west to meet with developers and talk with cottage owners. When he returned, he was so enthusiastic about the concept that he hung out a new shingle: the New England Cottage Company.

Two years later, he was still trying to get his first cottage project off the ground.

Although this kind of compact housing caught on more than a decade ago in the Pacific Northwest, Mirrione was unable to persuade tradition-minded New Englanders to give it a try. Zoning regulations made no allowance for this level of density, typically somewhere between twelve and thirty-six cottages per acre. And the suburbanites he approached made it very clear they intended to keep it that way. So, after being turned away in Easton, as well as the neighboring towns of Mansfield and West Bridgewater, Mirrione decided to do what many a persistent, mildly ticked-off Massachusetts developer has done before him: he tried to force a cottage plan through in Easton under Chapter 40B, the perennially controversial state law that gives a considerable edge to developers who set aside some housing for low- and moderate-income residents.

This was not the route Mirrione wanted to take. "We're not after McDonald's workers," he said at the time. "We're after the young professionals just out of college who might otherwise leave Massachusetts if they can't afford it."[4] He was aiming for a market-price range between $250,000 and $340,000, considerably less than the $392,500 median sale price for traditional single-family homes in Easton at the time. (The median subsequently declined with the recession and then, in early 2012, bounced back up above $400,000.)[5] But for his first project, Mirrione decided, he would have to work within the strictures of 40B, pricing about a quarter of the cottages at around $145,000 for income-restricted buyers.[6] He needed the affordable-housing law as a battering ram through rigid zoning and the thinking behind it. "The attitude in these towns is, 'I've got mine and I don't care about anyone else,'" says Mirrione, a gregarious, barrel-chested guy with a neatly trimmed mustache. "After I explained to people in Mansfield how cottage housing would fill a need, I had a guy look me right in the eyes and say, 'I don't care.'"

The strategy might well have worked were it not for the deep and prolonged national recession. Mirrione and his partners had spread themselves (and their investors' money) too thin across several other planned developments brought low by the housing market crash.[7] By 2011, Mirrione was bankrupt, his cottage plans dashed. But he wasn't wrong about the concept's viability. Since then, at least three other developers have managed to successfully pull off small cottage developments elsewhere in Massachusetts and in Rhode Island. With support from town officials, they were able to do what Mirrione could not: prove to skeptical suburbanites that density, if done right, can be not just tolerable but even desirable.

PEOPLE WHO LIVE IN Easton (pop. 23,000) refer to two Eastons: North and South. North Easton gets all the attention because it's the end associated with the Ames family, operators of a famed nineteenth-century shovel factory. "Easton in essence was owned by the Ames family for a century or so," says Chuck King, a former selectman. Stone factory shops that once comprised the world's largest shovel company, employing some five hundred workers at its height, still stand in the heart of a village once teeming with workers.[8] The tenements that housed many of those workers are gone now. But the village's artful layout remains, along with the many architectural demonstrations of the Ames family largesse, like the granite library and a grand meeting hall with an arched arcade, both designed by the prominent architect Henry Hobson Richardson. One former Ames estate, Wayside, now houses the town hall. Another became what is now Stonehill College.

If the Ames legacy blessed the north end with lasting cachet, South Easton missed out. "Any townie will tell you, North Easton got the library and the college, and South Easton got the dump," says Joseph Conforti, a semi-retired airline pilot who moved to a house in the south end in the 1990s. The sense of superiority in North Easton is so palpable that parents there rose up in anger a few years back when the school committee decided to mix elementary students from both ends of town in the same school.[9]

Mirrione hoped to bring South Easton some notoriety of its own as the place where modern-day cottage communities made their New England debut. He kept the sites he'd selected quiet at first, not wanting to create a distraction before he'd removed the primary barrier to these projects. He needed to persuade the town to ease up on its one-acre zoning for single-family homes. Mirrione went before one town board after another to pitch the cottage concept, each time stressing its importance as a way to provide "starter" homes. He called it "gap housing," homes that would help fill the affordability void between prices and incomes. His target market consisted of the people earning between 100 percent and 130 percent of the area median income. (As of 2012, the median in Easton was about $104,000, as determined by the US Department of Housing and Urban Development.) Surprisingly, even though home prices had fallen considerably since the height of the market boom, that income bracket still wasn't enough to comfortably afford the average home in Easton, or in many other suburbs, for that matter. In fact, in three-quarters of Greater Boston communities a median-priced single-family home wasn't reasonably affordable for those households earning the median income.[10]

Smaller houses could be less expensive but only if they didn't require much land. As Mirrione explained, "If I have to pay $200,000, $250,000 for a house lot, I have to build something large to make it profitable. But we don't need more four-bedroom houses. If I can get seven small houses on an acre, and get my land costs down to $30,000 to $35,000 a unit, then I can build something people can afford."

He proposed a new zoning bylaw, one that would allow Easton's planning board to grant a special permit for cottage housing. The bylaw set precise parameters for what such developments should look like. It allowed for up to seven cottages per acre, but no more than thirty cottages in one development. Cottages could have only one or two bedrooms. Architectural design standards, inspired by

New England sensibilities, stipulated front porches, pitched roofs, fences, and decorative walls. Landscaping guidelines required that at least a quarter of the tract be set aside as common land, with specified types and numbers of plantings.[11]

Some town officials liked the idea—the affordable housing board, Planning Board, and selectmen officially endorsed the bylaw.[12] "I hadn't heard of cottage housing before Nick brought it to our committee," says Rachel Hansen, then a member and former chairwoman of Easton's Fair and Affordable Housing Partnership. "We thought it was a creative solution to providing housing at lower price points."

In the minds of many more Easton residents, however, density plus tiny houses equaled a 1970s-style subsidized housing project. When the bylaw proposal hit the floor of the town meeting in May 2007, one voter after another, including the conservation commission chairman, stood up to decry cottages as a threat to the water supply, the schools, and the overall character of the town. Some critics seemed to have no understanding of the concept. "When we think about Easton and why we live here," said Mark Carpentier, then a member of the Finance Committee, "one of the things we like is that Easton is not a sprawling suburb."[13] That was precisely the point of cottage housing—to concentrate housing in built-up areas, rather than spreading it across open land. But Easton was just not interested in trying something new. "It was like we were coming in and saying, 'Guess what? There are computers now!'" Mirrione jokes. In the end, he goes on, "We got slaughtered. We were trounced and held up like drug dealers outside of schools."

To be sure, Mirrione was motivated by self-interest—the cottage concept was potentially a lucrative niche. An up-by-his-bootstraps conservative, Mirrione wasn't in the development business for the feel-good factor. "I want to build something that people need and is going to sell," he said. "This is how I make a living." But he was firmly convinced that cottage housing could be a part of the solution to the state's affordability problem. He figured that just one model cottage project would open doors in other communities. So, he decided to take route 40B directly through Easton's zoning blockade.

His tenacity won approval from the *Boston Globe* (a paper he usually loathes for its liberal editorial slant). "Mirrione simply wants to build homes that are attainable," read a *Globe* editorial. "But there is little room to negotiate with overwrought opponents who greet even a simple cottage development as if it were a teeming slum."[14]

This, as it turned out, was a very accurate description of the reception Mirrione received once he disclosed his planned development sites early in 2008. He'd selected two South Easton sites, both on major travel routes and, importantly, within densely developed areas identified by the town's own affordable-housing committee as appropriate for such housing. Each location was to have twenty-eight cottages, seven of which would be priced for income-restricted buyers. The site Mirrione would focus on first was a 3.74-acre property on Pine Street, a cut-through street lined with homes.

The plan came as a most unwelcome surprise to the street's residents. "They're using 40B as a gun to hold this town up so they can make a fortune," charged Gregory Roman, who'd only moved to Pine Street from Providence, Rhode Island, two years before. "Putting twenty-eight homes on just under four acres of land is crazy." A commercial film director, Roman and his business partner ran a production company out of their home, a 1940 brick schoolhouse that had been cleverly converted into three apartments. Black wrought-iron gates block the driveway—Roman had them put in because too many people were parking in his yard to get to the ball field in back. But all in all, he said, living in Easton was "idyllic" compared to the noise he used to put up with in the city.

A shady sanctuary from the commercial development and busy roadways all around it, Pine Street was lined with an eclectic meld of homes that, in an era of orderly subdivisions, came across as refreshingly arbitrary. An early-twentieth-century bungalow claimed four acres next to a two-family on a lot a quarter of the size. Postwar ranches and Capes with above-ground pools and concrete walks were interspersed with antique homes hugging the roadside. Amidst it all sat a tractor-trailer yard. There wasn't any obvious reason why Pine Street couldn't absorb cottages into its miscellany, provided, of course, that the development could meet septic and safety standards. And single-family home neighborhoods were a far better location for cottage clusters than were areas where tall, blocky buildings would overwhelm the diminutive structures.

But Roman and other neighbors just couldn't fathom the density. In a letter to the editor of a local newspaper, Roman called the cottage housing plan a "glorified trailer park."[15] In conversation, he went further to say that Mirrione was creating a "mini-ghetto." Black-and-white signs appeared up and down Pine Street: "Save Our Neighborhood" and "Stop 40B." It didn't help that the proposed development site, at 121 Pine, had come to be viewed as a farmyard of sorts. Neighbors said the woman who'd lived in the modest white farmhouse there kept about a dozen goats and some geese until she passed away. "The grass was all kept low and mowed from the goats," said Cecilia Mahoney, a hairdresser who lives in a century-old colonial across the street. The goats didn't bother Mahoney; the prospect of twenty-eight cottages did.

As soon as the cottage plan began to make its way through the approvals process, Mahoney established herself as a staunch opponent. She laid out her concerns in a neatly printed letter to the Zoning Board of Appeals, which was reviewing the cottage application. She spoke out at public hearings and online in a popular community forum. Her long list of potential pitfalls included water runoff, septic failures, increased traffic, and decreased pedestrian safety. But her main gripe was what she termed "extreme density," a condition she clearly associated with lower-class, urban areas. "We're not against affordable housing. We're against cottages and we're against density. The people who live in the large houses in subdivisions in North Easton—this isn't going to go in their neighborhoods," Mahoney complained, invoking the time-honored Easton class divide. "We kind of feel like it's being shoved on us."

At one public hearing held in the high school auditorium, Mahoney nervously stood up to tell officials she hadn't moved to Easton thirteen years ago for this. "I grew up in Dorchester [a neighborhood of Boston] in a house with nine kids," Mahoney said. "I know what it's like to have density."

PEOPLE ARE DRAWN TO suburbs not only for what they offer, but for what they leave out. This is as true now as it was in the late nineteenth century, when American suburbs emerged as dwelling places apart from increasingly crowded and dirty cities.[16] Separating ourselves from the city separated us from much of what made us uncomfortable—rapid change, noxious industry, a steady influx of immigrants, a fading agrarian ideal. Suburbs became a domestic balm for an anxious people. Even today, in areas surrounding thriving, dynamic cities, the American psyche still largely perceives spread-out suburban neighborhoods as more wholesome, closer to the land.

"Our cities and villages were dense for a mere 150 years before losing population to the suburbs in the middle of the twentieth century," write Julie Campoli, a planning and design expert, and Alex S. MacLean, an aerial photographer, in their book *Visualizing Density*. "We're accustomed to a lot of space between our neighbors and ourselves."[17] And embedded in this bias are a host of negative associations with what people generically refer to as density. As Campoli and MacLean point out, typically, what people really object to is crowding, noise, and congestion. Density is not necessarily synonymous with all of those things. The cottage-housing concept, done appropriately, is meant to be the antithesis of all that can go wrong with density.

"Bad" density is what began to drive people out of cities during the industrial age, when living conditions took a turn for the worse. Tenements crammed with immigrant workers sprang up around factories, sometimes so close together that city population densities surpassed a hundred thousand people per square mile.[18] On the outskirts of the growing cities, developers promoted the green landscape beyond as a morally superior and healthy alternative to disordered, dirty urban living. In Boston, the well-to-do rode the expanding and expensive commuter railway out to planned residential preserves, like Brookline and Chestnut Hill, but it wasn't until the emergence of the streetcar in the late nineteenth century that commoners could afford to move outside the city limits. And because the poor were left behind, moving out was also considered moving up.[19]

The societal anxiety around rapid industrialization and rising immigration only served to heighten the country's age-old obsession with the farmer and the frontier. By the end of the nineteenth century, as New Englanders began to wonder whether the industrial cities thriving along the rivers would overtake the region, northern communities were exploiting those fears by pitching rural vacations as an antidote. In 1899, New Hampshire governor Frank Rollins hatched a promotion called Old Home Week. Designed to link country towns with sentimental images of home and childhood, Old Home Week invited visitors to partake in simple, homegrown events like parades, church suppers, picnics, and band concerts. Eventually, all the New England states adopted this new "tradition."[20]

In 1926, the US Supreme Court affirmed the assumed evils of high-density environments in *Euclid v. Ambler*, the landmark decision validating zoning as a tool for separating incompatible uses. The case involved a landowner in the village of Euclid, a suburb of

Cleveland, who wanted to develop industry in an area zoned for residential use. The court upheld the municipality's legal right to regulate land uses and to separate industry from housing. But significantly, the court went further to target multifamily housing as incompatible with single-family neighborhoods, even though both uses are residential. The decision famously compared apartment buildings to "a mere parasite, constructed in order to take advantage of the open spaces and attractive surroundings created by the residential character of the district."[21] The derisive tone was echoed in lower-court rulings, in which judges implied a cause-and-effect relationship between multifamily housing and "crime, fire, dirt, noise, disease, low morals, and congestion."[22] Fear of such housing—or, more precisely, its occupants—pervaded many suburban communities, perhaps most acutely among the elite. Even earlier, in 1912, after the Massachusetts Civil League warned that wooden "triple-deckers" were spreading "like the cholera or yellow fever," Weston, Massachusetts, already an exclusive enclave, passed an ordinance banning all "tenements."[23] Although Weston had little experience with multifamily housing, the committee that promoted the ban warned that apartments would attract "a class of tenants who add nothing to the revenues of the town, but who, on the contrary, become the cause of increased expense in all departments."[24]

After *Euclid*, suburban communities quickly adopted zoning aimed at preserving their single-family flavor. The rise of the automobile enabled what Christopher Leinberger has aptly called "drivable sub-urbanism," or low-density growth, encouraged by federal supports for single-family home loans and highway construction.[25] Meanwhile, in center cities, high-rise public housing projects were going up in the name of slum clearance and urban renewal. In their book *American Apartheid*, Douglas Massey and Nancy Denton argue that urban "renewal" wound up destroying more housing than it replaced and had the effect of further concentrating blacks in ghetto areas, away from white areas. By 1970, "public housing projects in most large cities had become black reservations, highly segregated from the rest of society and characterized by extreme social isolation."[26] Often badly maintained and devoid of amenities, the high-rises became the housing of last resort. The tenant population became poorer and tended to have more problems. Alan Mallach, a veteran planner, author, and housing consultant, stresses that, contrary to popular opinion, not all projects were failures. Although public housing has been much maligned, many housing authorities have successfully provided "decent, safe environments to many of the poorest Americans."[27] But the most troubled projects received the most attention, and assumptions that the people who lived in public housing were morally inferior persisted. Suburbia was firmly established as a refuge from the deviant ways of the disadvantaged.

In 1969, a Cape Cod resident who feared that her small-town haven was about to be invaded by the urban poor penned a scathing letter to Massachusetts state senator John "Joe" Moakley. "The fact that they cling together in the cities is that living is easier and they haven't got the guts to go out on their own," she fumed. "This is what creates slums. It has always been and always will be until you can make laws forcing people to live like human beings instead of pigs."[28]

Her anger with Moakley, who represented South Boston, stemmed from the senator's efforts to break down the walls of restrictive suburban zoning. A few years earlier, the suburban voting districts had handily supported legislation calling for desegregation of the state's "racially imbalanced" schools. This caused turmoil in city neighborhoods—and was strongly opposed in Moakley's own Irish American working-class district—but left the almost exclusively white suburbs untouched.* Moakley joined with lawmakers

---

* The Massachusetts Racial Imbalance Law was passed in 1965.

from other urban areas to craft legislation that would force suburbs to lower their own barriers to economic and racial diversity. The new law was designed to provide a way around zoning laws that effectively blocked low- and moderate-income housing.

"Our fortunate citizens living outside the city have almost re-awakened colonialism," Moakley said in a speech on the Massachusetts State Senate floor. "They work and derive revenue from our cities, but leave it at night to enter their heavens."[29] Opponents responded with charges that the bill was un-American, socialistic, and a violation of home rule.[30]

Moakley and his allies were successful nonetheless, and the law he helped usher into being is what is now known as 40B, or, the "anti-snob zoning law." Since its passage, 40B has generated some fifty-eight thousand housing units, about half of which are considered affordable.[31] The law works like this: In any community where less than 10 percent of the housing meets the state's definition of affordable, developers may sidestep local zoning and seek a single comprehensive permit for projects in which at least 25 percent of the units are set aside for low- to moderate-income households. If a community's Zoning Board of Appeals rejects the permit application, or approves it with what might be construed as unreasonable conditions, the developer may appeal to the state Housing Appeals Committee.

Most 40B applications are negotiated and approved at the local level, avoiding the state appeals process.[32] But this is as much a reflection of increased sophistication about the limits of the law as an indication of municipal acquiescence. Although 40B regulations have been significantly revised in recent years to, for example, curb project sizes and rein in developer abuses, its encroachment on the same sorts of exclusionary barriers Moakley sought to breach remains fiercely controversial.[33] Efforts to repeal 40B surge every so often—the last one, in 2010, drew significant support from voters in Easton.[34] Anti-40B sentiment, and

objections to affordable housing in general, are still largely derived from the same old fears and prejudices around density, says
Bob Engler, a Brighton, Massachusetts–based affordable-housing
consultant who wrote his master's thesis on 40B at the time of its
passage. "In Colorado, people don't mind density as long as they
can see the mountains," Engler says. "Here, the suburbs are afraid
of multifamily housing. I call it Natty Bumppo-ism, this desire to
keep moving away from development."*

Massachusetts is trying to coax towns to embrace density by
offering monetary bonuses to those who zone for high-density
"smart growth" areas. A carrot alternative to 40B's stick, the bonuses offered under that law, Chapter 40R, had resulted in 33 smart
growth districts as of the end of 2011.[35] Looking ahead, both 40R
and 40B could function as crucial counterweights to the Bumppo
syndrome. If Massachusetts is to grow and thrive, it needs to generate more housing suitable for the young adults who are crucial
to its future. The state's home prices continue to act as a barrier
to young talent, even after the housing collapse. Homeownership among those twenty-five to thirty-four years old declined by
nearly 20 percent toward the end of the last decade, considerably
more than the national decline. Some of the drop-off is explained
by a shift to renting, but a larger portion reflects the state's shrinking supply of young adults.[36] Not unlike the rest of New England,
Massachusetts lost more than 5 percent of its under-forty-five
population over the last decade. That pace is matched only by some
struggling Midwestern states.

"A divide is emerging between areas of the country that are
gaining young people, and those in which the up-and-coming

---

* Natty Bumppo is the hero of James Fenimore Cooper's Leatherstocking
Tales series of novels, published in the early 1800s. A skilled white fron-
tiersman who was raised by Native Americans, Bumppo rejects civiliza-
tion in favor of the vanishing wilderness.

generation is shrinking," said a recent report from the Brookings Institution. This national unevenness renders the Northeast more vulnerable to the costs of aging, which, the report noted, include diminishing tax bases and slower-growing labor forces.[37]

A separate study by Barry Bluestone, the founding director of Northeastern University's Center for Urban and Regional Policy, links the state's declining young-adult population and lackluster job growth to its high housing costs. Increasing the supply of housing that is affordable to young adults could be a key economic development strategy but one that will require more creative approaches to density.[38]

THE TRADITIONAL NEW ENGLAND village, the pride of many a community, was laid out in a way that was both dense and orderly. Homes, offices, and shops coexisted in a compact arrangement that usually incorporated a green. The architecture tended toward neoclassical, and the paint preference was for pristine white. That we still find these historic villages so pleasing today has to do with qualities that Campoli, of *Visualizing Density*, associates with "good" density: varied, interesting architecture; connection to a neighborhood; walkability; a sense of identity; green space. And yet many New England communities have effectively zoned out this sort of living. "We have made it illegal to build anything so dreadful as a Kennebunkport [Maine]," jokes Edward Moscovitch, president of Cape Ann Economics, in Gloucester, Massachusetts.

Linda Pruitt, the owner of Seattle's Cottage Company, counts many of the qualities of "good" density as hallmarks of her own developments. Of the seven cottage developments Pruitt's company had built at the time that Mirrione was pursuing his plan, all had sold out. This is not to say that cottage living is meant to suit everyone. (Pruitt herself prefers a remodeled three-bedroom home

from the 1950s.) But it is a choice that meets the needs of a significant segment of the population—that small-household segment.

In the Seattle area, proponents of cottage housing have had an
easier go of it because political will is on their side. In 1990, the
State of Washington passed one of the most progressive—and controversial—land-use laws in the country, the Growth Management
Act. An attempt to slow sprawl and protect the environment, the
act requires fast-growing counties and cities to write local plans
that protect environmentally critical areas but also encourage development in designated "urban growth" areas. "Cities and towns
were mandated to create certain numbers of housing—they had to
grow," Pruitt explains.

Since then, as part of their growth plans, many Seattle-area
municipalities have adopted cottage bylaws. The concept has not always worked, and in fact has sometimes gone horribly wrong. The
city of Shoreline, about fifteen miles north of downtown Seattle,
halted new cottage communities in 2006 because of neighborhood
objections to what city planning director Joseph Tovar described
as several "bad" projects. The city's cottage ordinance proved too
flexible and allowed for developments that were too close together,
skimpy on common space, or raised too high relative to the rest of
the neighborhood. "The biggest issue that mattered was context,"
Tovar said. Now, however, other communities considering cottage ordinances can build on the experiences, good and bad, of the
past. The website of the Municipal Research and Services Center of
Washington includes links to cottage bylaws and offers guidelines
for drafting an ordinance.[39]

Seattle has experimented with allowing construction of backyard
rental cottages as a way of generating more affordable housing.[40]
Many Pacific Northwest cottage communities are geared toward a
more affluent segment of the market, however. Ross Chapin, an architectural champion of so-called "pocket neighborhoods" who has

partnered with Pruitt on some projects, prides himself on building
to such high standards that his cost per square foot easily exceeds
the average for single-family homes.[41] Pruitt too is consistently focused more on quality and design than affordability. Her buyers
tend to represent an educated backlash to the McMansionization of
single-family homes; they may be able to afford larger homes but
want to live in a more environmentally friendly way, Pruitt says.
"People want longer-lasting materials, lower energy costs—something of a European model, if you will," she explains. And compared
to single-family homes, cottages are both a more efficient and less
intensive use of land. Fewer people live in cottages than in the traditional single-family home, and fewer cars come and go. "If you consider four single-family homes versus eight cottages on one lot, the
tendency is to automatically think four is better than eight," Pruitt
says. "But our experience shows that eight cottages will have the
smaller impact."

IN LATE 2008, STANDING before an audience of skeptics in Easton's
state-of-the-art high school auditorium, Mirrione again sought to
ease fears of density, this time with a PowerPoint presentation. He
included photographs of the colorful and lushly landscaped cottage
communities he had visited in the Seattle area. These were obviously not mobile homes—they were stick-built in place, like any
other house. Shots of the cottage interiors demonstrated how high
ceilings and well-placed windows created an open, airy feel. Outside, individual driveways were noticeably absent; walking paths
connected the Cape Cod-styled homes.

Alas, the fairy-tale effect did not quell suspicions that Mirrione
was out to ruin the neighborhood. After the public hearing, Cecilia
Mahoney said that, while the cottages pictured looked attractive
enough, she suspected the camera angles made them look bigger

than they are. And the cottages might not look so good once they'd aged a bit. "I think it's going to look like a really cute trailer park/ condo community," she said. "I've named them 'tondos.'"

Another Pine Street neighbor, Joe Conforti, the pilot, was there to film the hearing. An amateur filmmaker, he said the cottage project had inspired him to make a documentary about 40B.[42] His feelings about the development were much like those of other Pine Street residents, who, in conversations after the hearing, said they felt violated by what they considered an unwanted intrusion on their street. Conforti offered an analogy: using 40B to get around zoning was akin to invading someone's home and smacking around their family.

If Pine Street residents felt abused, before long, it became obvious that Mirrione was feeling some pain himself. The still-sinking housing market was dragging his development company down with it. Property values were tumbling, and projects that once looked profitable no longer penciled out. Banks began foreclosing on properties Mirrione and his partners had slated for development.[43] In some cases, Mirrione tried to beat the banks to the table by selling off properties on his own. Even as he abandoned some projects, he continued to pursue the cottage initiative. Asked by reporters about his company's financial status, Mirrione expressed confidence in his ability to survive the downturn, which he predicted was nearing an end.

Instead, conditions only worsened. In June 2009, Wells Fargo bank began foreclosure proceedings on the Pine Street property. Still Mirrione insisted that the cottage project would be built, "and it's going to be built by me."[44] Although he'd laid off almost everyone in his office, he continued to pursue a comprehensive permit.

The Zoning Board of Appeals eventually granted that permit, in February 2010, three years after Mirrione first began pitching the cottage concept. But it was too late. Wells Fargo now owned the Pine Street lot. Two months later, Mirrione filed for bankruptcy, claiming $18 million in liabilities. It was an ignominious end for a project Mirrione had pursued with such enthusiasm. Or was it? "I still think someday it will happen," Mirrione said in early 2012. Because the permit runs with the Pine Street property, he was still hopeful that he could reacquire the land and revive the project neighbors hoped was dead.

If cottages had proved too much for Easton to handle at the time, strangely enough another plan for high-density housing had found favor in town—and in, of all places, North Easton.

The fifteen, mostly vacant buildings that comprise the former Shovel Shops in the heart of North Easton's historic village had been targeted for affordable housing, also under 40B. The developers planned to demolish some of the industrial buildings and add on to others. This so alarmed Ames family descendants and preservationists that they got to work on a plan of their own, one that would capitalize on the factory's historic value and enhance the village's nearby commercial district. The factory buildings would be restored and converted to 113 apartments, 20 percent of them affordable.[45] A 2.4-acre public park would be incorporated into the development, along with a museum to house Shovel Shop artifacts.

Beacon Communities, the Boston-based multifamily housing developer, stepped in to champion the project and worked out a partnership arrangement with town officials. Easton voters, faced with a much denser project under the 40B proposal, chose to support Beacon's plan with a $4 million loan from Community Preservation Act funds.[46] A $43-million undertaking in total, the project will, in essence, both revive and memorialize high-density functionality in the village. In the words of Beacon's CEO, Howard Cohen: "If you think about North Easton and the historic sites that are there . . . you will have one of the most architectural, landscaped, historic town centers in the country."[47]

Easton was rewarded for its initiative. The state Department of Housing and Community Development has since turned away a developer seeking 40B eligibility for a project in Easton, citing in part the town's measurable progress in creating housing opportunities on its own.[48]

MIRRIONE WAS NOT THE only New England developer to become entranced with the cottage housing concept. Others too were pursuing projects, and in 2011, cottage developments popped up in several locations. In Concord, Massachusetts, Dan Gainsboro of NOW Communities built a "green" cottage community off Main Street, adjacent to the Assabet River. Based on a site plan designed by Ross Chapin, Concord Riverwalk consists of thirteen homes on two acres with an adjoining two acres of open space. The cottages are crafted from high-efficiency materials, outfitted with energy-saving appliances, and prewired for solar-panel electricity, should owners choose to go greener. The Riverwalk is not entry-level eco-consciousness: prices for two- and three-bedroom cottages start at around $600,000.

In contrast, a cottage project in Westford, Massachusetts, was conceived as affordable from the start. Howard Hall of Cottage Advisors (a developer of seasonal cottage communities) and David Guthrie of Wescon approached the town about partnering on affordable housing. The town put up some land, and the developers came up with a 100-percent affordable project. Cottages in the Woods is to have twenty two- and three-bedroom cottages priced between $150,000 and $168,000 for income-qualified buyers. Though construction was slowed by the recession, four of six cottages completed as of mid-2012 had sold, according to the Westford Housing Authority.

A third cottage community, in East Greenwich, Rhode Island, is a blend of affordable and market-rate homes. Five of the fifteen homes lining either side of a courtyard at Cottages on Greene are restricted for moderate-income brackets. The below-market cottages sold for $165,000 to $235,000; two went to single women in their thirties looking to buy their first home. The rest of the cottages, which are about a thousand square feet, are priced just under $300,000.

Gaining town buy-in on the development wasn't difficult given that the one-acre downtown site was previously covered with junk cars, says the developer, Leonard Iannuccilli. Although the recession slowed the pace of sales, and diminished profits, Iannuccilli, who runs a real estate agency in East Greenwich, says doing cottage housing, in this case with architect Donald Powers, was one of the more satisfying experiences he's had in thirty years in the business. Here was a project that finally made sense. "For years I'd been working with developers doing subdivisions with super-size homes," he explains. "I used to say, we're building homes for people who can't afford them, with money they don't have, to impress people they don't know. You could just see it—it was stupid."

THREE

Pride and Prejudice: Milbridge, Maine

T HE PEOPLE BEHIND MAINE'S "The Way Life Should Be" cam-
paign obviously never set foot inside one of the state's sea-
cucumber factories. Preparing the slimy brown cucumbers for
human consumption is a revolting process that requires slashing
open the creatures and scraping out the meat. Confronted with bin
after bin of the tubular blobs, workers in the factories spend their
days slashing and scraping as fast as they can.

Mainers certainly aren't known for shying away from hard and
unpleasant work. But even the hearty have their limits. When a
sea-cucumber factory opened in a small Down East coastal town in
the late 1990s, the locals kept their distance. Located in Milbridge
(pop. 1,300), a village so far northeast of the lower Maine border
it's closer to Canada, Cherry Point Products had previously pro-
cessed sea urchins. But as that fishery declined, the owners, Lawrence and Drusilla Ray, invested in the equipment necessary for
processing the previously shunned cucumbers for Asian markets.
Figuring into their calculation was the rural area's desperate need
for jobs—but they failed to consider the "ick" factor. As Drusilla
once explained it, the work "was dirty. It was cold. It was wet. It was

repetitive. It was smelly. It was—how many adjectives are there? It was everything that was not appealing."[1]

When the locals failed to line up for the work, the Rays turned to an alternative labor force, one known for taking on tasks that native Mainers have come to avoid. They recruited Hispanic migrant workers, the laborers who travel by the thousands to Maine every summer to help with the harvest of the state's star indigenous crop, wild blueberries. Maine is the world's largest producer of the tiny, tart fruit, most of which is harvested in sprawling Washington County, where Milbridge is located, on the thousands of acres of flat, sandy plains known as "barrens."[2]

Harvesting wild blueberries was once a grassroots Down East affair, a seasonal cash-making opportunity. Come late summer, kids and adults alike would hunch over the low-lying bushes for hours, sweeping up berries with a "hand rake" that looks like a dustpan with teeth. So many schoolteachers and students took to the barrens every summer that if the harvest lasted into September, local schools sometimes didn't open until the raking was done.

By the 1980s, however, blueberry growers large and small were hiring more migrant workers. The community-raking tradition broke down as young people drifted away for greater opportunities, and retirees from away moved in. Native Americans, who had long rounded out the ranks of white rakers, dominated the barrens for a while, but gradually, more Hispanic migrants, mainly from Mexico and Central America, found their way northward.[3]

The Rays tapped into the migrant network to recruit factory employees. They set up a trailer park for them to live in and only charged for utilities. In the course of three years, the Rays were employing dozens of migrant workers. The jobs that repelled locals had the opposite effect on migrants—many viewed the work as a good reason to stay put. They settled into Milbridge with their families and enrolled their children in the public schools.

Life in rural Maine took some getting used to. "The small store in town had like two jalapenos, two peppers, and three tomatoes," recalls Edith Flores, whose family was among the first to settle in town, in 1999. "We started asking the store manager to bring more. Then we'd all call each other when he brought in a pound of jalapenos." But the town's small size, quaint village center, and remoteness appealed to workers tired of chasing crops up and down the coast. Situated at the mouth of the Narraguagus River, its jagged outline formed by rocky shoreline and quiet coves, Milbridge felt surprisingly humble for a place of such natural beauty. Life in Milbridge was "peaceful" compared to Florida with its "racists," one Latino worker told a reporter.[4]

Like many of the locals, the migrant families managed to piece together enough work between the Rays' factory, the blueberry harvest, and other seasonal jobs like wreath-making to support themselves year-round. By the time of the 2000 US Census, almost 7 percent of Milbridge's residents identified themselves as Hispanic, distinguishing the town as one of the most racially diverse communities in one of the whitest states in America.[5]

If locals found the influx unsettling, they mostly kept it to themselves. "Things were maybe a bit touchy with local people at first," Drusilla Ray told *Down East* magazine in 2008, by which time her factory workers had been assigned another disgusting fish, the very aptly named slime eel. "Now [the Hispanics] have become accepted."[6] It was as though the town's tranquil setting had set the tone for smooth cultural relations. The elementary school hired a teacher to help the new students improve their English. The downtown BaySide market rearranged its shelves to make room for Goya products. At community potlucks, baked beans rested easily alongside burritos. And perhaps most surprisingly, on Main Street, in front of a small white house, a sign went up reading Mano en Mano (Hand in Hand). Founded by a social worker and a nurse practitioner, the organization provided a space where Hispanic newcomers could find help with everything from learning English to filling out paperwork to math assignments.

The picture looked all the more serene when compared to the nearby city of Lewiston, which had absorbed hundreds of Somalian refugees, beginning in 2001. A city of thirty-six thousand, Lewiston's initially warm reception had quickly iced over as the number of refugees topped a thousand. That was when Lewiston mayor Laurier T. Raymond Jr. wrote an open letter to the Somalis of Lewiston asking that they discourage others from following. "We have been overwhelmed and have responded valiantly," the mayor wrote. "Now we need breathing room. Our city is maxed-out financially, physically and emotionally."[7]

The letter offended local Somalis, who accused the mayor of bigotry. The mayor's defenders accused the Somalis of trying to take over their city. When a white supremacist group showed up, anti-hate activists shouted them down. The national media captured it all.

In contrast, the media had come to Milbridge to showcase the remarkable absence of shouting and demonstrating. In 2006, a *Washington Post* reporter juxtaposed "the placid coexistence" of immigrants and locals in Milbridge against the divisive immigration debate in Washington. Perhaps in an area of Maine this removed, the reporter mused, "people don't get excited about anything."[8]

Silence does not necessarily equal acceptance, however. And soon enough, it was obvious that one had been confused with the other. Within a couple of years of the *Post* article, Milbridge had divided in two. On one side were those who were supportive of their immigrant neighbors and on the other those who'd decided they were a financial burden. A petition circulated. Neighbors made ugly remarks in public. And Mano en Mano, crying discrimination, sued the town in federal court.

It turned out that even the good people of Milbridge could get excited about some things. And one of those things was affordable housing.

Six modest apartments, to be exact.

IDENTICAL BRIGHT BLUE CABINS are lined up like Monopoly houses out at the rakers' camp in Deblois. It's early evening, and as workers trickle in from the miles of blueberry barrens, their collective fatigue is as palpable as the drizzle hanging in the air. It has stooped their shoulders and drained the vigor from their chatter. But a lone worker has begun to kick a ball around the soccer pitch in the middle of camp. Soon, a match will be underway. Fatigue will not deny the workers their nightly *futbol*.

The wild blueberry, like its crustacean counterpart the lobster, has come to be synonymous with "real" Maine. Yet the migrant workers who pick them have not, even though migrant worker camps like this one are a seasonal fixture on the Down East landscape. This camp just outside of Milbridge is run by Wyman's, short for Jasper Wyman & Son, a privately owned corporation founded in 1874. Headquartered in Milbridge, Wyman's owns thousands of acres of barrens and purports to be the largest US supplier of wild blueberry products. Off-season, Wyman's employs about 135 full-time workers at its processing plants in Deblois and Cherryfield. But at harvest time, when the factories run round-the-clock to clean and freeze about a million pounds of blueberries a day, Wyman's employs some 600 workers out in the barrens and in the packing plants. The company also provides free housing at this camp, which includes 75 cabins, a new dormitory that sleeps up to 150 men, and camper sites with electrical hook-ups.

The workers are divided into crews that begin raking as early as 5 a.m. They are paid by the box: $2.25 for 23½ pounds of fruit. Average pay for experienced rakers (some of whom are still locals) comes to about $1,500 a week, according to Nat Lindquist, Wyman's vice president of operations. "But in a good field," he adds, "I've seen a raker do 300 boxes a day." Even the fastest rakers can't compete with the mechanical harvesters Wyman's now uses to bring in more than half of the crop. Improvements in mechanical harvesting equipment have resulted in sharp reductions in the ranks of hand rakers—and may someday replace them entirely. But for now, Wyman's can't do without them.

On this gray evening, a stocky fellow in a white t-shirt stands lapping a strawberry ice cream cone outside a canopy stretched between two camper trailers. Bare bulbs are strung beneath the canopy and glow dimly on a dozen or so men eating at picnic tables. The men are mostly quiet, their focus on a television perched in one corner of this makeshift café. A sandwich board outside reads Vazquez Mexican Food. The stenciled lettering is in red and green, the colors of the Mexican flag.

The man with the ice cream cone is Gosafat Vazquez, the proprietor of this establishment along with his wife, Romana. They are not migrants—they live in Milbridge and were among the first Hispanic workers to take jobs at the sea-cucumber plant, in 1998. About a decade ago, Romana figured she could put her superb cooking skills to better use and opened a Mexican food concession in an old bus next to their home in town. A customer suggested they might find an even more receptive audience at the Wyman's camp. With the permission of management, the Vazquezes now park their camper kitchen here every August, reviving weary rakers with spicy tamales, fat gorditas, beef tacos, and, for Americanized tastes, cheesy fries.

Originally from Mexico, Gosafat speaks little English, but he is happy to chat, with help from his daughter Susi. Susi, an eighth grader with long hair tucked back in a bun, is the youngest of six Vazquez children and one of five girls. She learned English in kindergarten and has since become an able translator.

She was just four months old when the family moved to Milbridge. They had been living in a small trailer in Florida and traveled up and down the coast to Michigan and Maine and back. In 1998, the Rays offered them jobs at the sea-cucumber plant and a mobile home to live in for $100 a month. That seemed like a good deal.

"Lawrence Ray is a good boss," Gosafat says. "He's helped us a lot." The factory work is no longer as reliable as it was at first. But now they have the food concession. And in 2004, Lawrence agreed to sell Gosafat the mobile home, which the family has since renovated and expanded.

Meanwhile, the grown Vazquez kids are carving out their own niches. Roberto, for example, has an auto shop next to their house. The oldest daughter, Juliana, spent several years working as a certified nursing assistant. She and her husband have since bought their own home, where she runs a day-care center. Another sister has her own painting business, and yet another has a cosmetology degree. In a town without much work, the Vazquez family has managed to find opportunity. This is home now, Gosafat says.

The adjustment was tough at first, Juliana will explain. She believes she was the first Hispanic student to attend the regional high school. And winter was a shocker: "We were like, whoa! It's so cold!" She and her sisters were often bored. "We stayed on the couch and we put our feet up and we were just thinking about what we should do. There was nothing around. In Florida, we used to go biking around. Here, we were afraid about going outside because we didn't know anybody."

But people in Milbridge turned out to be welcoming and gradually made the family feel at home. Juliana has settled in so well that the day-care center she runs is full, with a waiting list. "The community is very close," she says, "and there is a lot of help around."

■　■　■

YOU MIGHT SAY IT was Christine Roberts who upset the cultural equilibrium. A farmworker-housing specialist for the US Department of Housing and Urban Development (HUD), Roberts was new to Maine in 2007. She'd transferred to Bangor from Florida, a state notorious for its use and abuse of Hispanic migrant workers. Maine was different—its farmworker population is much smaller and more fluid than Florida's. And Maine employers have a far better reputation for their treatment of farmworkers. But substandard and insufficient housing for these workers is a chronic problem, and Roberts aimed to deal with it.

Accurate numbers are hard to come by, but suffice it to say that thousands of migrant workers appear in Maine every year to gather apples, broccoli, and berries come harvest time. Most are part of what's known as the Eastern Migrant Stream, a migration pattern that runs from Florida to New England. Many of these migrants use Florida as a "home base" during the winter. Their transient lifestyle and low incomes make it difficult to find decent housing, both at home and on the road.* So when they're working, many depend upon their employers to provide them with a place to sleep at night.

During blueberry season, workers who don't arrive in time to claim an employer-provided cabin or dormitory cot may wind up bedding down in cars or tents. "They often just find a place to camp themselves," says Arthur Emerson, a pastor with the Downeast Maine Mission's Migrant Ministry. "It's difficult for all of the growers to have camps for them because it's too expensive to meet state standards for employee housing that is only needed for a few weeks a year."

On one of her first Down East tours of worker camps, Roberts had visited some decent employer-provided housing. But she had

---

* The median monthly income for migrant farm workers was $860 as of 2000, according to a survey by the Housing Assistance Council.

also seen some trailer camps that barely met the definition of shelter. One camp owned by a grower stuck in her mind. Fiberglass insulation hung from the ceilings of the trailers, and electrical wiring stuck out from the walls. In the overcrowded bedrooms, tenants had strung ropes and hung them with curtains of clothes for privacy. It was winter when she visited, and the frigid air followed her inside the trailers through broken doors and ill-fitting windows.[9]

Migrant workers looking to settle in Washington County—which, as of the 2010 census, had around 450 Latino residents—face the same housing-affordability problem as the locals. Competition from summer people and retirees has sent land values soaring: home prices in the Down East region climbed by nearly 60 percent between 2000 and 2006. Although values have dropped considerably since the housing crash, as of 2009, an estimated 45 percent of households in Washington County were still unable to afford the median-priced home.[10] Rental options are limited, unless you're looking for a summer cottage. Most towns have fewer than a hundred year-round rentals each (Milbridge has closer to 120), and monthly costs are notoriously burdensome.[11] An astonishing 70 percent of Milbridge households can't afford a basic two-bedroom apartment without spending more than 30 percent of their gross income.[12]

Landing a rental at Milbridge's only affordable-housing complex, Saybrook Apartments, can take years. The wait list for one of the fourteen garden-style apartments usually stretches to at least fifty names.[13]

Roberts saw subsidized housing for settled farmworkers as a way to relieve some financial pressure, improve the stock of decent rentals, and help stabilize a workforce that supports some of Maine's oldest indigenous industries. When she came to Maine, no one had ever built this type of housing before. The US Department of Agriculture provides grant money to finance construction—Roberts just needed to find a nonprofit willing to apply for it. Competition was stiff. The total money applied for typically equals three or four times the amount of funding available.[14] But Roberts thought it was time Maine gave it a shot, especially since the housing would accommodate such a broad segment of the local workforce.

Under federal guidelines, anyone who derived substantial income from aquaculture, agriculture, or the handling of those commodities was eligible. That would mean the housing would be open to blueberry rakers, fish processors, clammers, lobster sternmen, wharfside seafood handlers, and the "tippers" who cut the balsam for the factories churning out holiday wreaths. Hispanic ethnicity was *not* a requirement for eligibility. US citizenship was.

Roberts asked around at various state and local agencies—who might be an appropriate sponsor? All pointed her in the same direction: Mano en Mano, Milbridge's tiny social service organization for Latinos.

Mano was not a housing developer. Nor had it ever aspired to be. Hispanic residents knew to go to Mano for help with homework, or filling out paperwork, or finding a doctor. Mano sent teachers out to the raker camps to work with migrant students and invited in the Milbridge community for multicultural potluck socials. Rooted in literacy classes and language exchanges that once took place at the town library, Mano sought to build bridges, not homes.

Nevertheless, Mano's board of directors agreed to hear Roberts's pitch. She didn't try to sugarcoat what the development process entailed—the hurdles were high, and community opposition was guaranteed. As generally welcoming as Milbridge had been to Hispanic newcomers, Roberts warned, proposals for farmworker housing often brought out the worst in people, eliciting anti-immigrant sentiments that escalated the usual panic about the "element" affordable housing brings in.

Roberts herself had borne the brunt of such fears of contagion when a nonprofit she'd worked for in Florida proposed farmworker housing in the town in which she lived. The proposed site for the development, a group of single-family homes to be called Hacienda West, had functioned as a buffer zone between some fairly expensive Spanish-style homes and a neighborhood of much more modest housing. People who lived in the high-end neighborhood did not want affordable housing across the street. And Roberts, an active parent volunteer in the Girl Scouts, her church, and the PTA, heard about it everywhere she went. The project would bring in drug users and alcoholics, other parents told her. It would bring in bad parents who didn't control their kids. It would destroy the value of surrounding homes, wiping out equity and ruining peoples' retirement plans. Some of these people were visibly angry when they unloaded on Roberts. It did little good to cite research refuting their claims—several studies looking at affordable housing's impact on property values have found no negative effect when the developments are of good quality.[15] Behind their anger, and even behind the overtly racist stereotyping, was what Roberts had come to recognize as an abiding fear of change.

Roberts also checked in with Milbridge's town manager, Lewis Pinkham. "I said, 'How would you feel if somebody were to try to develop some housing for farmworkers?'" Roberts recalls. "Part of Lewis's answer was he really felt that the Hispanic farmworkers were important because the local folks weren't raking the blues anymore or tipping the wreaths. He called it repopulation—that was the word he used."

At the time Mano's board decided to take on the housing project, the organization's executive director, Anais Tomeczsko, was fairly new to the job. Originally from Philadelphia, Tomeczsko was a recent graduate of the College of the Atlantic, a small school in Bar Harbor, Maine, that caters to idealists out to change the world. When she'd started working with Mano, she says, she'd been "floored by the ability of most of the local population to see things as they really were and not through the lens of bias. I met these salt-of-the-earth fishermen who would talk to me about how hard-working and family-oriented Latinos were."

For all its virtues, however, Milbridge was not immune to racism. Tomeczsko had comforted children who had been spit on by other kids for speaking Spanish on the school bus. So, although she saw housing as an obvious need, Tomeczsko anticipated some ugly pushback. "Anais could see it coming," says John Wiltse, a veteran developer of farmworker housing, mainly in New York, who acted as a consultant to Mano. "There were folks who wanted these people to disappear at the end of their workday and not be part of the community." But neither Tomeczsko nor Wiltse expected the full-on firestorm that lay ahead.

THE BACKLASH BEGAN ALMOST the instant Mano made its plans public in 2008. A petition arrived in Pinkham's office signed by forty-eight residents. They wanted to stop the "low-income complex" planned for property on Wyman Road, at the edge of the village center. Their stated reasons included concern that the values of nearby properties would suffer and that low-income residents would burden town resources. And then there was this:

"We know the lobster industry is threatened with the added cost of fuel and all it brings. We wish to protect any jobs they may need in the future, not to be given out to minorities that may move into these units."

Daniel H. Pride, a retiree who lives across the street from the development site, says he started the petition. Formerly a manager for Scott Paper, Pride is from lower Maine, but come retirement, and after trying out Texas, he moved Down East to find reasonably priced property not too far away from water. The island on which he'd grown up has been given over almost completely to summer people, who can afford to pay a half a million or more for a house.

He couldn't live there now, but doesn't hold that against the sum-mer people—they spend a lot of money locally and keep up their properties nicely. "It all went to the better," he says.

In Milbridge, he found a fixer-upper and worked on the house himself. Wyman Road is a fairly tight enclave of fishermen, which suited him. Running along the shore of Narraguagus Bay, the road is home to many families whose ties to lobstering go back genera-tions. In fact, his next-door neighbor, Lena McKenney, was born and brought up on Wyman. Her father, grandfather, and great-grandfather were all lobstermen, and McKenney herself hauled traps for a while, back when few women were doing such work.

It was McKenney who called and told Pride about the "low-income apartments" going in across the street. He'd gone right down to see the town manager, Lewis Pinkham. Lewis, he'd said, what's going on here? And Lewis told him it was Mano en Mano, they wanted to set up some housing for the immigrants coming in. "I said, 'Lewis, I don't think the town is set up to take on this bur-den. And being on Wyman Street, this is an all-fishermen street. This just doesn't fit the neighborhood and doesn't fit the town.'"

Most of Pride's Wyman Road neighbors agreed, as they will-ingly signed the petition. A lot of them struggle themselves, he says. The folks in the house at the end of the road are so bad off that they use a blue tarp for a roof. These local people have made their own way. "And it bothers me that we don't take care of our own," he says. "I've been on Social Security for seven years and I've never had an increase. It's getting harder to live. And they keep throwing money around to help immigrants."

The financial insecurity described by Pride has a long history in Milbridge—and in Washington County as a whole. Life there has been hard for so long that endurance is less admired than it is expected. "Local people are hard laborers. There are no soft-jobs here," says Pride's neighbor McKenney. She is a case in point. She says her work life began at the age of fifteen in one of the sardine factories in town. (The last sardine factory in Milbridge closed in 2000; the last in Maine shuttered in 2010.)[16] She hauled traps by hand during her lobster-fishing days but had to stop because of back problems. At the age of forty-seven, she embarked on a new career with a degree from cosmetology school. Now in her sixties and still bothered by back problems, McKenney continues to run a hair salon out of her house.

The scant thirty-three thousand people who live within Washington County's 3,255 square miles largely derive their living from the bounty of natural resources: the sea, the barrens, the timber, the rivers. But some of the most sustaining industries from the past—shipbuilding, sardine canning, commercial fishing—are gone or in decline. (Lobsters remain one of the more reliable fisheries.) Full-time employment is harder to come by—most people piece together seasonal jobs, like clamming, digging bait worms, and wreath-making. Hard work doesn't always add up to a living, however. Some 20 percent of county residents live in poverty, the highest percentage of any county in the state.[17]

Economic stagnation has bred demographic stagnation. Washington County lost 3 percent of its population over the last decade, even as Maine's population as a whole grew by 4 percent, according to US census figures. Youth and young adults are leaving, passing incoming retirees and seasonal homeowners on their way out.[18] Compared to other Maine counties, Washington County has one of the highest proportions of senior citizens in the state.[19] Not surprisingly, given its age and income level, the population here is also more dependent on the government—transfer payments (mainly Medicare, Medicaid, disability, and retirement benefits) represent nearly 36 percent of personal income.[20]

In the regional school district that includes Milbridge, the absence—not the excess—of children is causing taxpayers pain. The state has drastically reduced its subsidy for local schools because it sees enrollment declining and taxable property values soaring. In short, by the state's calculus, the district doesn't need as much aid because it is land-rich and student-poor.

"That's been a hard pill to swallow for people," says Ron Ramsay, the superintendent for the six-town district. "They've watched individual property taxes skyrocket. We have families who own very modest homes that happen to be on the water that have to pay $6,000, $7,000 a year in taxes. A lot of them sell out and move inland. They sell to someone who can afford it. And then those people probably don't have kids—they come in and complain about taxes too."

Ramsay has welcomed the appearance of Hispanic children in the district's schools. He figures that, by adding to the headcount, those kids have probably generated more revenue for the district (through state subsidies) than they cost it in English-as-a-second-language services (one teacher's salary, at about $30,000).

By the same token, the Hispanic migrant workers represent replenishment of the younger workforce, the workers needed to support existing businesses and create or attract new ones. Not that the numbers of those who have settled in the county have been nearly enough to level off the decline. Based on current death, birth, and migration rates, the state projects a continued loss of population in a half-dozen Maine counties, including Washington, over the next twenty years.[21] As the *Bangor Daily News* reminded Milbridge residents in an editorial questioning objections to Mano's proposed housing project, the new Latino residents "give the region what much of eastern and northern Maine desperately needs: population growth."[22]

But Mano's project proved to be the catalyst for people who were angry about a lot of things to get vocal about one thing. If the sources of their anxiety were rising property taxes, scarce employment, and insufficient Social Security payouts, the immediate targets were affordable housing and immigrants. Some of the opposition smacked of a "why them and not me" mentality. Reaction was similarly bitter when the TV show *Extreme Makeover* set up in Milbridge to redo a home for a local family on Wyman Road, recalls Nat Lindquist, the Wyman vice president. Then, critics questioned whether the family's economic circumstances really warranted such charity.

With the farmworker housing, opponents also questioned why certain ethnicities were entitled to free housing. Ignoring the waves of nineteenth-century immigration that brought many of their own French-Canadian and Irish ancestors to northern and eastern Maine, some even suggested that the Latinos, like the apartment building, did not "fit" with this town. And it wasn't until April 2009, when Tomeczsko walked into a room filled with about seventy mostly unhappy residents, that she realized just how hot an issue the housing development really was.

THE PETITION HADN'T REALLY surprised Tomeczsko—she had expected some NIMBYism. And otherwise, the project had seemed to be proceeding smoothly. Mano had won a $1-million housing grant from the US Department of Agriculture, a feat that John Wiltse considered a minor miracle. Town officials had also given the project a boost. At Mano's request, the selectmen had signed an application for a Community Development Block Grant that Mano put toward the cost of preparing the five-inch-thick USDA application.

The development plan was modest: six apartments in a single two-story building. Half would have two bedrooms, and the other half would have three. All would have a single bath and an open kitchen-living-dining area.

Tomeczko had signed a purchase-and-sales agreement for the land, a five-acre lot. She didn't anticipate any zoning conflicts— outside the shoreline zone, Milbridge barely had any zoning restrictions at all. The project would have to comply with a subdivision ordinance, but that hadn't posed a problem for two other subdivisions approved on Wyman Road in recent years. And the lot was plenty big enough to support a private well and septic system.

It looked to Tomeczko like she'd made it over the major hurdles—right up until she caught wind of a meeting about the project, organized by the selectmen, and without her knowledge. The speaker was Bob McCurry, with the USDA's Rural Development Agency. He'd been asked to attend the meeting to answer the community's questions about the housing project. But as Tomeczko watched, the Q&A deteriorated into a siege.

In addition to the usual complaints about traffic and noise, some residents stood up to complain that immigrants were taking jobs. Some suggested that Latinos were likely to pack as many people into these apartments as possible, and that their children would burden the schools. Neighbors of the project said they feared it would attract drugs and crime.

Discontent only grew after McCurry acknowledged that, because Mano was a nonprofit organization, it would not pay full property taxes on the project. Instead, it would make some yet-to-be-determined payment in lieu of taxes.[23]

Tomeczko could hear people commenting in the background, and their remarks alarmed her more than the public back-and-forth. Someone murmured, "We could always get a can of gas and take care of it." Then, a quiet threat, heard by both Tomeczko and a Mano board member: "If you build it, we will burn it down."

By the end of the meeting, it was clear that the project was in trouble. Tomeczko had thought that town manager Lewis Pinkham was in her corner, but now she had serious doubts.

Within days, town officials were discussing a moratorium on multifamily housing development. Pinkham said the moratorium would give the town time to improve its land-use regulations—and Mano's project would have to be put on hold in the meantime. Mano had its fair share of supporters but not enough acted to turn the tide. At a special town meeting, Milbridge residents voted 68 to 49 to enact the moratorium for six months, with the possibility of renewal.

The moratorium was potentially fatal to Mano's project. A prolonged holdup could cost them their federal grant. If they lost the grant, they would lose the $80,000 they'd already invested in the project. And they also stood to lose the five-acre development site if the owner chose not to renew their option to purchase.

"Our hands had really been tied," says Tomeczsko. "The town was responding to this kind of vocal minority. Maybe they felt like they had no choice. But we felt like they acted pretty rashly and quickly."

Mano's board didn't believe that the holdup was grounded in concerns about land-use regulations or traffic. They believed the moratorium was rooted in prejudice.

In July 2009, with the help of attorneys working pro bono, Mano filed a federal lawsuit alleging discrimination under the Fair Housing Act and the equal protection clause of the Constitution. The once welcoming town of Milbridge now stood accused of enacting a multifamily housing moratorium "out of fear that Hispanics and Latinos would move into the development or to appease citizens who had similar fears."[24]

LEWIS PINKHAM IS THE man at the fulcrum of Milbridge affairs. A Down East native with a moustache and wire-rimmed glasses, Pinkham is smaller in stature than one might expect for a man who carries so many titles. In addition to being town manager, Pinkham is also the chief of police, town treasurer, code enforcement officer, welfare director, and road commissioner. If you have a problem in Milbridge, chances are that Pinkham is the guy to see. He can be found in the somewhat decrepit town hall, at the back of a warren of cramped offices, surrounded by files and boxes and maps.

"Lewis has a deep understanding of things," says Candace Austin, one of the founders of Mano en Mano (but no longer with the organization). When Spanish-speaking residents began to settle in Milbridge in greater numbers, he helped ease their entry into the elementary school by encouraging a program of diversity education. He'd further opened up cultural communications by providing his police and fire staffs with Spanish language cheat sheets. "Lewis began the community cultural events with me," Austin says. "He was trying to put together people who were interested in helping him rise to the occasion."

For all his skills as an intermediary, however, Pinkham was unable to squelch the outcry over Mano's housing project. Now that the controversy has died down, he downplays its significance, saying that, overall, he is "very pleased with the way the people I grew up with have accepted the diversity in this town." The way he sees it, Mano's claims of discrimination were overblown. Yes, some people behaved badly at that meeting with the USDA official, he acknowledges. As police chief, he might have liked to arrest them for their racist remarks, he says, but "fortunately, in this country we have the right to free speech, no matter how stupid it is."

Pinkham maintains that much of the anger stemmed from poor communication on Mano's part, that the agency pursued the project without first building the necessary support among various factions in the community. "There was very little of that whole process that was because of culture and race. The majority of it boiled down to dollars and cents: property taxes," Pinkham says. Milbridge already has another agency that receives breaks on taxes—the Washington Hancock Community Agency, a social service organization. "And the more of those you have," he continues, "the less revenue you have coming in, and it shifts the burden on everyone else." Mano's current executive director, Ian Yaffe, agrees that "taxes were a major issue that just wasn't dealt with early enough."

But then again, sometimes objections to property taxes are the acceptable cover for deeper prejudices. Dick Fickett knows this from experience. Born and raised in nearby Cherryfield, Fickett dedicated nine years to getting the Saybrook Apartments built. Much of that time he was battling a small minority of opponents—even though his project, as a private enterprise, would (and does) pay taxes. "There's a perception of affordable housing as what they see on TV—a junk property, gangs, drugs," Fickett says. "They can't say those things in a public meeting, so they say, 'How are we gonna afford those kids? How are we gonna deal with all those cars?'"

Did town officials institute the after-the-fact moratorium in response to those spoken and unspoken prejudices? Pinkham says no—it was imperative that the town write an ordinance tailored specifically for multifamily projects. "We tried to assure the folks at Mano en Mano that it was never our intent to inhibit the building," he says. "But they accused us of using this to put them off so they would quit."

As the lawsuit hit the newspapers and the controversy heated up, quitting sometimes looked tempting. Says Wiltse, "There were moments when Anais and I were like, why the hell did we get into this? But Anais is tenacious, and some board members dug in their heels."

The town was also feeling the pressure. HUD began snooping around. Further, the Civil Rights Division of the US Department of Justice filed an amicus curiae brief in Mano's case that laid out the legal precedents for linking the actions of municipal officials with discriminatory sentiments in the community. Based on previous rulings, Mano "need not establish that each selectman, and each town resident who voted for the moratorium acted with discriminatory intent," the division's lawyers said, "only that the national origin or familial status of the prospective residents, or both, was a motivating factor in the town's decisions."[25]

Town counsel warned publicly that if HUD determined that Milbridge was in violation of the Fair Housing Act, the town might face a fine or have to repay past grants.[26] Then, Mano won an important victory: the judge in the case ordered the town to allow the housing project to continue moving through the approval process, pending a verdict.

Perhaps town officials recognized that the momentum was not going in their direction. By November, five months after the moratorium vote, a new land-use ordinance was put in voters' hands and quickly approved.

The town had officially removed its blockade. Tomeczko lauded the move as "a step in the right direction." But Mano did not immediately drop its lawsuit. "They can't violate the Fair Housing Act . . . and pretend nothing has happened," said April Bentley, one of Mano's lawyers.[27] Still, some on Mano's board wanted to end the acrimony. It would be several months before the two sides reached a settlement agreement. In the end, the town's insurer paid more than $25,000 for Mano's legal fees.

Resentments in the community continued to fester. In December 2009, two men drove up to the Milbridge home of a resident from Honduras. There, one of the men, twenty-five-year-old Sherman L. Merchant from Steuben, fired four rounds into the house.

He and the Honduran fellow had been involved in a car accident earlier in the day. According to court records, Merchant later told people that he planned a payback for "the Mexican," whom he alternately referred to as a "nigger."[28]

One of the bullets fired at the house hit the victim in the shoulder, but he was not seriously harmed. Merchant was convicted on several charges and sentenced to prison. But the crime also came under separate scrutiny—the state attorney general's office deemed the action a crime of prejudice and filed a complaint under Maine's Civil Rights Act. The resulting court order prohibits Merchant from ever again abusing the victim or any other person for reason of race or color.[29]

Meanwhile, Mano pressed on. And in October 2010, more than two years after they'd received their USDA grant, the agency finally began clearing land for the new Hand in Hand apartments.

ON A SUNNY JUNE day in 2011, Ian Yaffe welcomed about a hundred people to the grand opening of the farmworker apartments. A recent graduate of Bowdoin College, Yaffe had replaced Tomeczko after she departed for a job in Colorado. He told me that he'd vowed not to become too familiar with the negatives of the past so that he could better focus on establishing positive relations. In that spirit, he had invited nearby neighbors on Wyman Road to the opening of the apartment house. And among the curious few who came by was none other than Lena McKenney. "Yes, ma'am, I did," McKenney says. "They were going to be my neighbors."

Standing at a podium before the guests seated in folding chairs in the parking lot, Yaffe described the two-story apartment building behind him as "an opportunity for families to stay in Milbridge, where they can enrich the community and foster our sense of place." Maine's Agriculture Commissioner, Walt Whitcomb, was also invited to the podium, where he talked about the importance of farmworkers to Maine's economy. "We are standing here in a place where truly weary workers will come to rest," Whitcomb said.[30]

Guests received a tour of the building, a colonial-style structure with a pitched roof and green clapboards. The entry foyer is painted a warm teal. A separate mudroom provides a place for workers to rinse off and store their dirty boots and outerwear. The apartments are bright, with energy-saving radiant-heat floors.

The total cost for the project had come in at around $1.35 million, higher than expected for a project with just six apartments.

The moratorium and delays had pumped up the project's cost by about $155,000 due to the expanded approval process under the new ordinance and construction inflation. (The price of the land had also threatened to rise as the process stalled. One of Mano's lawyers solved that problem by buying the property himself and then later selling it to Mano.) Mano managed to piece together the additional funds through low-cost loans from USDA and Coastal Enterprises, a local community development organization. In order to cover the additional debt, Mano had to set rents at a higher rate than expected, but the USDA was making up the difference. Tenants would still pay no more than 30 percent of their income.*

The rent structure also allowed Mano to make a substantial payment in lieu of taxes. "It put a lot of folks' minds at ease," Pinkham says. Yaffe had assured him that Mano would try not to burden the town. As of the end of 2011, the two sides were negotiating a multiyear payment agreement.

The other major objection by opponents—that Latinos alone would receive cheaper housing—has not come to fruition. In fact, at first, Latino families were slow to show interest in living there. Dick Fickett is managing the property for Mano. He says one family backed out because the rent seemed too high compared to the trailer they were renting. Another was wary of having to provide information about every family member or friend who might come to stay with them. The one-year lease is also a bit of a deterrent to families used to being free to move on when jobs become scarce.

---

*John Wiltse, the housing consultant, is quick to remind those who grumble about the use of tax dollars for rent subsidies that the federal government also subsidizes homeowners by allowing them to write off the interest they pay on their mortgages. Because of the way the mortgage deduction is structured, the largest benefits accrue to high-income Americans with expensive homes.

The units were rented to both Latinos and local people, some of them married to each other. Lena McKenney knows two or three of the families there—"They're decent folks." The apartments haven't brought in the crime and sleaze she expected. In fact, having a rental building across the street hasn't caused her any trouble at all. She's still not happy about it, but she's resigned.

"I've just kind of grown used to it," McKenney says. "No different than any other place. It has to grow on you."

FOUR

Shifting Lines in the Sand: Watch Hill, Rhode Island

A TAIL-LIKE EXTENSION OF Rhode Island's southwestern tip, the spit of sand and gravel known as Napatree Point gracefully curves off toward the horizon, a wide-open pathway into the sea. Its entire mile-and-a-half length is barren of development, save for the century-old ruins of a fort used briefly as a coastal defense lookout. A hump of grassy dunes runs down Napatree's middle. On one side, a broad beach faces the open Atlantic; on the other, a rockier shore forms a protected harbor within Little Narragansett Bay. The view from atop the dunes or from Napatree's rocky tip takes in a spectacular three-state panorama that grazes the shores of Block Island, Long Island, Fishers Island, and Stonington, Connecticut.

Part of the historic village of Watch Hill, in the town of Westerly, Napatree is both shorebird preserve and public beach. Nature foiled long-ago attempts to civilize its shores. The devastating Hurricane of 1938 wiped out an entire cottage community along Napatree, killing many of its inhabitants.[1] The storm also amputated the farthest reach of Napatree, forming an island known as Sandy Point. Without so much as an ice cream vendor now, the

"Naps" is a no-frills idyll as popular with beachcombers as with birds. The peninsula's long reach into the bay also makes it an anchorage mecca for boaters looking to get to shore. On a sunny summer weekend afternoon, the back side of the spit often resembles a motorboat parking lot. "You go up and down the shore and there are not many places where you can anchor," says Fred DeGrooth, a charter captain who has lived in Westerly for about twenty years. "So people anchor in Little Narragansett Bay, take their inflatables to Napatree, and walk to town."

About 90 percent of Napatree is owned by the Watch Hill Fire District, an unusual quasimunicipal authority chartered in 1901. Fire districts in New England are commonly separate taxing districts that pay for and maintain their own fire departments. The Watch Hill Fire District, however, has additional powers that give it considerable control over valuable real estate within its extremely affluent borders. Under its state-approved charter, this fire district may buy and manage property. In addition to a firehouse, the district owns prime beachfront and precious parking lots in the village's small commercial strip on Bay Street. The district also owns and runs the Watch Hill public beach, bathhouse, and the antique "Flying Horse" carousel.

If some of its property, like the harborside park on Bay Street and the Watch Hill beach, is accessible to the public, much of it is reserved for and leased to private entities. These include the members-only Watch Hill Yacht Club in the harbor, as well as the yacht club's beachfront cabanas, and the Misquamicut Beach Club, a shorefront extension of a highly selective nearby golf club. The self-serving aspect of this arrangement has not gone unnoticed—a state lawmaker once accused the Watch Hill fire district (and two others like it in Westerly) of holding onto beach properties as a means of "exclusion."[2] Watch Hill residents' usual response to such criticisms is to wave their sizable property tax bills, a reminder that the high property values in their desirable district are a boon to town coffers.

Surrounded by water on three sides, Watch Hill has served as a summer resort since the nineteenth century, when polite society began coming by steamer to escape the city heat and while away the season in rambling wooden hotels. "The visitors to this place represent annually the choicest class of society," reported one newspaper correspondent in 1868.[3] Gradually, the wealthy built their own "cottage" colony, laid out by a Cincinnati syndicate whose members were all summer people. They carved a 130-acre farm into house lots and controlled the sales so as to shape a colony where, according to one Watch Hill history, "one could meet only the 'best' sort of people."[4] Today, newer money, much of it flowing from Wall Street, competes with older, pedigreed wealth. Private homes have replaced the old hotels, though some of the "cottages" are of nearly hotel-size proportions.

Visitors of lesser means have long found Napatree Point to be one of the more accessible features of beautiful Watch Hill. Gaining admission to the peninsula's beach has simply demanded that you are able to get there. On foot, that means walking through a public parking lot off Bay Street and then around the private beach club's fenced parking lot to the Naps's narrow pedestrian entry path.

In the summer of 2007, however, the policy of unhindered access to the point suddenly began to change. First, a big green sign appeared at the trail entrance. Use of the point is "permissive," the sign said, "but permission may be withdrawn at any time for any purpose."[5] Visitors were advised that they could not bring in beverages, not even bottled water. Nor could they bring their dogs, unless it was early morning or after 6 p.m., and then only on leashes. This came as a rude surprise to dog owners. A town ordinance similarly prohibited dogs on public beaches, but the rule had never been enforced on Napatree.[6]

A gate went up—not locked, but off-putting nonetheless. Hired wardens began patrolling the dunes, watching for violators. Then smaller signs, dozens of them, popped up in the grass warning visitors of the importance of dune protection and the hazards of ticks. Ropes were strung across the many pathways over the dunes.

Napatree, it turned out, was now a threatened-species zone. The Watch Hill Fire District, along with another Napatree parcel owner, the privately funded Watch Hill Conservancy, had signed agreements with the US Fish and Wildlife Service authorizing the agency to manage the federally protected piping plovers and least terns common to the point.[7] Fish and Wildlife's role was to rope off and monitor areas where plovers were nesting in the sand. The fire district and conservancy had taken it upon themselves to hire the wardens and put up signs.

This new arrangement was necessary, the groups said, in order to protect Napatree from overuse. Conservancy officials pointed to a study they'd commissioned that concluded that extensive human (and canine) use was harming the dunes, along with the well-being of threatened birds like the plovers. For years "there had been no monitoring of human activity out there," says Chaplin B. Barnes, a lawyer and the executive director of the conservancy. It was, he says, "a wild land." So, upon the conservancy's creation by some Watch Hill property owners in 1999, one of its top priorities became working with the fire district to protect Napatree.

If preserving Napatree was a laudable goal, the locals who regularly roamed its shores were not convinced conservation was the sole aim. "There was a sense that somehow the conservancy and the fire district were trying to exclude people," says Steven Hartford, Westerly's town manager. The warning that "permission may be withdrawn at any time for any purpose" sounded to some like a threat. This did not sit well for two reasons. First, for all the money and power behind them, the conservancy and the fire district were not town enforcement authorities. Second, although the fire district owned most of Napatree, and the conservancy a slice, in addition to some privately owned lots, pieces of the peninsula were also assigned to the state of Rhode Island and the town of Westerly.

The daytime ban on dogs, even when leashed, sparked special fury.* "What do we have here, a bunch of dog haters?" demanded one angry Westerly resident at a town council meeting.[8] Some Watch Hill business owners said disappointed tourists were complaining.[9] Even some Watch Hill residents questioned the ban—discreetly. In a letter to the chairman of the Watch Hill Fire District's park commission, Thomas W. Smith, a successful investor and regular Napatree dog walker, politely suggested that perhaps the village authorities were overreaching. "Placing a guard with a big Conservancy badge on his sweatshirt at the entrance of the Point is a very clear statement—plovers first, your dog-walking (on leashes, of course) constituents second," Smith wrote. "Moreover, is it appropriate for the Conservancy to become a law enforcing agency, even if to protect the plovers?"[10]

Many Westerly residents posed the same question, which the town solicitor answered without equivocation: no.[11] With public pressure mounting, the Watch Hill groups backed off a bit. The threatening language on the sign ("our goof," acknowledges Grant Simmons III, the chairman of the fire district's park commission) was removed, along with the gate. However, the rest of the rules, multiple signs, and a hired team of wardens and naturalists remain. The team keeps careful count of human visitors and dogs, and logs all rule infractions by type and frequency. They also count boats anchored in the bay and measure water quality. All of this information goes into a database, which Barnes says may at some point "tell us we need to do something differently."

---

* Leashed dogs are allowed at any time between Labor Day and May 1.

However, he fiercely objects to suggestions that the close monitoring of Napatree is intended for any purpose other than to protect the environment. "No one has ever been kept off that beach by anybody," he declares. What's more, adds Simmons, the fire district goes out of its way to accommodate the public, spending some $60,000 a year on cleanup and conservation efforts on the point. "We don't stop someone from going out there," he says, "but we tell them what the rules are."

And those rules still rub raw for some. The resentment is in part because the plover site on Napatree brings the number of plover projects in Westerly to four (counting Sandy Point), more than any other town in Rhode Island. But the broader concern is shore access, an issue that has been fraught with conflict here at least since the late 1970s, when six fishermen were arrested for trespassing while cleaning up debris along the several miles of beach between Watch Hill and the moneyed enclave of Weekapaug. What has come through in the current debate is that for many people, Napatree the "wild land" symbolizes something vitally important and increasingly scarce: unfettered access to a spectacular shoreline.

Rhode Island's constitution guarantees generous rights of access to the shore, "including but not limited to fishing from the shore, the gathering of seaweed, leaving the shore to swim in the sea and passage along the shore."[12] Those rights derive from the ancient public trust doctrine, which holds that the seashore belongs to all citizens, and that the ocean and some portion of the coastline below the high-water mark are held by the states for public benefit.* But as private interests have bought up and exerted more control

---

* This is a general description of the public trust doctrine, which dates to Roman times. Some states and their constitutions interpret public shore rights more liberally than others. In Massachusetts and Maine, for example, public rights to use the land between the high and low tide lines are more restricted than in Rhode Island.

over waterfront property, and the population vying for access has grown, conflicts over beach and water rights have become a constant tension in Rhode Island, as in coastal communities all over the country. If the ribbon of shoreline that is regularly covered by the tide is technically open to all, private property often blocks the way. Oceanfront property owners fearing trash, liability, and a loss of privacy frequently warn away outsiders with "no trespassing" signs and fencing, even near pathways officially designated for public access. In one of the country's more famous and protracted beach battles, DreamWorks cofounder David Geffen erected gates to prevent the masses from using a public pathway alongside his California oceanfront compound on Malibu's Carbon Beach.[13] On the New Jersey shore, whole towns have developed reputations for keeping people out by making it nearly impossible for them to park.[14]

Outside of the crowded beaches specifically reserved for the public, finding a way onto the open shore isn't always as easy as one might think—even in Rhode Island, the state with the license plate tagline Ocean State. The truth is, even though the ocean is considered a public resource, "the vast, vast majority of people are restricted to a tiny bit of the coast," says Robert Thompson, chair of the University of Rhode Island's department of marine affairs.

Already feeling squeezed, then, it's no wonder that Napatree devotees (and their dogs) object to now having to move over for nesting plovers.

IF WATCH HILL IS part of the sprawling beach town of Westerly, one is not to be confused with the other. People with summer homes in Watch Hill do not invite friends to come visit them in Westerly. Westerly grew up around granite quarries and mills, and has the heavily Italian and Irish population to show for it. The town's busiest beach, Misquamicut State Beach, with more than a half-mile of frontage on the Atlantic, supports a noisy array of motels, breakfast joints, surf shops, and miniature golf courses. Watch Hill, on the other hand, is hedgerow society and a yachtsman's paradise. Tourists too come to sample Watch Hill's island-like setting and long stretches of sandy beach. Many summer residents view tourism as a nuisance—"too many boats in the harbor" and "too many people on the beach" are longstanding complaints.[15] So, though Watch Hill accommodates day-trippers, it does so on fairly rigorous terms.

Driving toward the heart of the village, at the water's edge, a visitor is likely to pass a flashing sign outside the fire station. "Excessive Noise Prohibited," it warns. "Motorcyclists Take Notice." On Bay Street, where yachts rock in the harbor, while visitors poke around the beachwear boutiques or savor an ice cream outside St. Clair Annex, teenagers in white golf shirts patrol the street in search of those who have overstayed their welcome. Bay Street parking is limited to two hours per day; violators face a hefty $75 fine. (Do not, as this author did, confuse two hours per day with two hours per space. If you park on Bay Street while visiting in the morning, then leave for several hours before returning to park in the street again, you will be ticketed nevertheless.) Daily rates for beach goers are available in a couple of privately owned off-street lots; these fill by mid-morning when the weather is fine. In addition to Napatree and the Watch Hill beach (which charges $8 per adult), portions of the privately owned East Beach are open to the public, via a state-sanctioned path at the foot of Bluff Avenue. Cars may not park here however—a sign even prohibits standing.

Cars are not allowed at all on the winding, hedge-lined lane leading to the picturesque Watch Hill Lighthouse; visitors must walk in—if they can find a place to park. Private associations see to the maintenance of the lighthouse and other cherished symbols of Watch Hill's Victorian-era beginnings. The carousel, left behind by a traveling carnival in the late 1800s, still revolves at the beach's edge and is so assiduously tended to that its caretakers have been known to balk at saddling up children in wet bathing suits.[16]

In and around the village, homes dating to the original summer colony have been lovingly maintained in such numbers that Watch Hill is listed on the National Register of Historic Places for its evocation of an era gone by. Positioned amid the rolling topography to capture the best water views, many of these handsome shingle-style houses have been in the same families for generations. "A lot of the homes that do change hands here trade within a family," says Simmons. "We don't have a tremendous influx of new people. It's the kind of place that has to be discovered." The demolition of some historic cottages in recent years has caused consternation among the old guard, who don't approve of the super-sized homes going up as replacements. But aside from snubbing the offenders, there is little they can do, because, surprisingly, Watch Hill lacks local historic district protections. Village officials have been cool to the prospect, largely because the town, as zoning authority, and not the fire district, would be in control of such restrictions.[17] Watch Hill, you see, prefers to take care of its own affairs.

The resort hotels that once accommodated summer tourists here have long since succumbed to fire, hurricanes, condo-ization, or other residential development. Only one resort remains, the newly posh Ocean House.

Perched atop Bluff Avenue, its broad porches facing the sea, the cheery yellow hotel is a stunning reproduction of the Gilded Age original that stood in the same spot for more than 130 years. While still at its height, the hotel was featured in a 1916 silent film, *American Aristocracy*, which poked fun at the staid summer crowd's pomposity.[18] Like an aging grande dame, the Ocean House grew decrepit with time and was loved nonetheless. Even in her final days, loyal guests excused the lack of air conditioning, the shower-less claw-foot tubs, and the slanting floors as charming idiosyncrasies. By the time the hotel's owners put her up for sale, the old gal was on life support.

In 2004, a Connecticut homebuilder, Richard R. Girouard, bought the twelve-acre property, reportedly paying $13.2 million. Girouard wasn't on a rescue mission—much to the horror of local preservationists, he wanted to raze the Ocean House and replace it with five luxury homes.[19] This news caught the immediate attention of Charles M. Royce, the mutual fund manager and president of New York-based Royce and Associates. In addition to homes in Greenwich, Connecticut, and Palm Beach, Florida, Royce (now in his seventies) owned a waterfront home within view of the Ocean House. He had summered in the area for two decades—his $2-million vintage yacht, the *Aphrodite*, is a familiar presence in Watch Hill harbor—and had invested heavily in real estate throughout the town.[20] Like many people in town, Royce viewed the Ocean House as a community asset and an iconic landmark; he couldn't abide its destruction. With help from Westerly officials and pressure from an incipient "Save the Ocean House" movement, Royce persuaded Girouard to flip the property to him.[21]

What began as a noble restoration effort, however, soon fizzled to a salvage operation. Experts hired to assess the project concluded that the hotel's compromised structure was beyond repair. So Royce decided that, with help from local investors, he would save what he could from the old Ocean House, then demolish it and build a painstakingly crafted replica in its place.

No change of such magnitude goes down easily in Watch Hill. While there were zoning issues to iron out with town officials, an even bigger obstacle loomed in the form of unhappy abutters. Neighbors had battled back a previous proposal to turn the Ocean House into a luxury resort, even though the man behind that plan, Frederick Whittemore, a former managing director for Morgan Stanley and the president of the Watch Hill Conservancy, was himself an insider. Royce, however, proved a better politician. Determined to ward off unpleasant litigation, he patiently formed the necessary alliances and methodically wooed the neighbors, eventually even co-opting their lawyer to come work for him. The resulting deal included four pages of restrictions and covenants on the Ocean House property. The detailed terms specify limits on the new hotel's size and number of bedrooms, and preclude neighborhood disruptions like an outdoor pool and noisy music after 10 p.m.[22]

The project moved ahead, and in spring 2010, after an official blessing by local clergy, the new Ocean House opened for business. Designed by Centerbrook Architects of Connecticut, the building's exterior is indeed a close replica of the original, with the signature curved-portico entrance, the mansard roof, the enveloping and spacious verandas. A project that had originally been pegged at $60 million came in closer to $140 million, however, as the new Ocean House wound up substantially larger than the old and includes twenty-three private residences. Memorable interior elements salvaged from the old hotel stand out, including the wood-paneled elevator cab and the massive stone fireplace in the lobby. Upon its opening, an architectural critic for the *Providence Journal* lauded the end result, gushing, "In every corner of the new Ocean House the spirit of the old Ocean House lives on."[23]

The luxury hotel's opening amid a deep recession caused many to question whether Royce the investment guru had made a colossal financial blunder. He would later confess to *Forbes* that he questioned his own sanity at the time.[24] The condominiums, intended to help ensure the project's viability, have been slow to sell. But the resort is gaining a following among those who travel in five-star circles. Online reviews from guests are increasingly glowing. Watch Hill society too approves of the hotel. "Ocean House is a tremendous contribution and they did it correctly," says Michael Beddard, the president of the Westerly Preservation

Society, a Watch Hill group. "There was no half-heartedness, no compromise on standards."

The new hotel is certainly a boon to Westerly's tax base. As of 2010, the Ocean House was the town's top taxpayer, paying about $670,000 in property taxes, "almost too good to be true," says Charles E. Vacca, the town assessor.[25]

For all of its contributions to the town's tax base, however, the new Ocean House magnifies Watch Hill's exclusive leanings. If the old Ocean House relied on the ocean views, cool breezes, and lulling sounds of surf to soothe guests, the new Ocean House strives for an updated Gilded Age atmosphere. Guests enjoy pampering at a full-service spa, exclusive access to a private club room with a zinc-topped bar, butlers on the beach, and fine cuisine made from farm-fresh ingredients selected by a professional "food forager." In-season room rates start at around $700 a night, with suites fetching more than $1,000 a night. The private residences are priced well above $1 million.

Toward the end of its tenure, the old Ocean House "was kind of a dump, but it was our dump," observes Michael Goldblum, a New York architect who has vacationed at Watch Hill for years. By definition, a five-star resort is out of bounds to a sizable portion of the population. The new hotel is all about decorum and separateness. Some serving areas are reserved only for guests. Restaurant prices are daunting, and the portions paltry by local standards. The average $23 price for entrees is "a tough pill to swallow when you're talking about six bites of food," read a review in *Rhode Island Monthly* magazine.[26] Says one former Westerly town official, "I think they've successfully alienated the locals with the small portions and cordoning off certain areas."

The hotel parking lot, once open to beachgoers for a fee, is now closed to the public. And the Ocean House beach is more elaborately demarcated. "It's kind of like having a neighbor with no fence versus a neighbor who puts in a hedge," Goldblum says. "Before, you knew you were on their beach but you knew it was okay. Now, there are psychological barriers: formalized chairs in a nice row, a tent with pina coladas at sunset or something. It's more of a structured environment into which you would feel weird plopping your towel down and sitting there."

Like the new Napatree, the new Ocean House feels less welcoming to some. Not that anyone's complaining much, mind you, given the tax revenue and job opportunities it provides. And Royce does liberally offer up use of the hotel's communal spaces to local groups, especially in the off-season. But there are those who eye the hotel's extreme upscaling warily, seeing it as another sign that powerful private interests are gaining more control over some of the town's most beautiful shoreline areas. "If you've lived here long enough, you can see it," says Randy Saunders, a self-described townie who owns a clothing store in Watch Hill village. "And I don't like it."

A FORMER CASEWORKER FOR the state Department of Children, Youth, and Families, Randy Saunders has plenty to keep him busy in retirement. He writes, sails, travels with his wife, goes to blues concerts, keeps tabs on his business, and spends time with his grandchildren. The passion that has consumed him over much of the last decade, however, is advocating for public access to the shoreline.

As a Westerly native, Saunders recalls the days when he could anchor his small boat in Watch Hill cove and wade ashore onto Bay Street without anyone saying a word. "Things were very casual and beachy," he says. Now, that same cove is so filled with moorings owned by the private yacht club and its members that anchoring isn't allowed—even though the cove is a federally designated anchorage area, technically open to all.[27] Intentionally or not, the yacht club has slowly created the illusion that the cove is private, Saunders says. He sees similar practices all over the Westerly shoreline: "Private Property" postings of dubious authority. Public rights of way that are blocked or stripped of official markers. The intimidating sign that appeared on Napatree.

Saunders speaks out regularly about these issues. In Watch Hill, authorities tend to brush aside his criticisms as paranoid and unnecessarily divisive. ("He's a very angry man," says Barnes, executive director of the conservancy.) They were not amused when Saunders began selling t-shirts reading "Free Napatree" at the height of that controversy. Saunders was simply "an obstructionist," declared one former fire district official, Robert J. Brockmann, in a letter to the local newspaper.[28] Saunders hasn't quieted down. He still views the summertime crackdown on Napatree as part of an unceasing effort by moneyed interests to control the shoreline, with the possible intent of limiting or at least discouraging access. Napatree has survived just fine until now—what changed, he asks? And keep in mind, he adds, that the Watch Hill groups never invited community input on how to establish a balanced conservation plan for Napatree. Rather, he charges, they slam-dunked their own plan.

Saunders agrees that the dunes need protection but believes that could be accomplished with far less hoopla. As for the plovers, Saunders doesn't see the sense in encouraging the birds to nest in what has historically been a high-traffic area during the summer months. So far, even with protections in place, plover production on Napatree has been erratic—2010 was a banner year, with twenty chicks fledged, but 2008 and 2011 were both duds, according to Erin King, a wildlife biologist with the Rhode Island office of US Fish and Wildlife.

The way Saunders sees it, "The whole Napatree experience has been ruined. Instead of being this very open, natural environment, naturally shared by humans and other animals, it is now littered with signs, fences, wardens, and a sense that if you walk in the wrong direction or step on the wrong piece of sand, there will be dire consequences." A policed Napatree seems more aligned with the interests of the Ocean House and its guests than the general public, he says.[29] The hotel has, in fact, adopted the point as a mascot of sorts, having partnered with a local winery to produce its own Napatree Point Cellars label.[30]

Barnes paints Saunders as a lone complainer, but he wasn't the only one who objected when, after the new Napatree rules went into effect, fire district officials proposed that a conservation easement on the property be given to the Watch Hill Conservancy. Under such an agreement, the fire district would retain ownership of its Napatree land, but the conservancy would have legal authority to enforce conservation restrictions there in perpetuity. According to Barnes, the easement was conceived as a precautionary measure—it would provide "a layer of official conservation protection" in case future fire district officials show less interest in protecting Napatree. But giving the privately backed conservancy authority over property owned by the voter-run fire district was a red flag for those concerned about public access.

"Napatree not only needs to be protected environmentally; it must also be protected for the good of the public," argued a charter captain and Watch Hill resident, Jack Spratt, in a letter of objection. "The WH Conservancy's mission does not speak to promoting public access and use of our beaches and waterway resources!"* Watch Hill voters ultimately defeated the easement by a narrow margin.[31]

Fred DeGrooth has also accused Watch Hill interests of overreaching in the boating column he writes for the *Westerly Sun*.[32]

---

* The conservancy's Articles of Incorporation, as filed with the Rhode Island secretary of state, describe its purposes as environmental preservation, maintaining the character of Watch Hill, educating the public, and acquiring property.

A member of the Westerly Yacht Club, the town's largest marina, set on the Pawcatuck River close to its outlet at Little Narragansett Bay, DeGrooth is particularly incensed by their recent efforts to establish buffer zones and setbacks around Napatree, thereby limiting the size of the anchorage area for boaters. Their stated concern, shared by US Fish and Wildlife, is the protection of fragile shellfish and eelgrass beds. But the proposed rules they drafted left a lot to the imagination, specifying that the newly restricted anchorage area, as marked by buoys, could "change from season to season, and within a season." The draft also identified the private conservancy as the entity charged with "regulation and limitation" of public recreational uses at Napatree.[33]

Although he knows that preservation of eelgrass beds is important for sustaining healthy fisheries populations, DeGrooth is openly suspicious of the Watch Hill groups' push for more control over the anchorage, an area where the general public has freely enjoyed access. "They're using the curtain of environmental protection for a completely different agenda," he charges. "They're not dumb. They're very slow, very methodical."[34]

Barnes and Watch Hill officials insist that the draft's reference to the conservancy as the authority overseeing public recreation was a mistake—presumably, like the wording on the Napatree sign. Such "goofs" are fodder for local critics, but Grant Simmons, of the fire district, has little patience for what he views as a misguided attitude among some in Westerly about Watch Hill being exclusionary. "It's based in paranoia," he says. "It's offensive." Growing angry, he lists all of the Westerly entities that benefit from the generosity of Watch Hill donors, including the local hospital and library. "We support all of these things in a big, meaningful way," he says. "There's a lot that we do that we ask nothing for. We do it very quietly."

The fire district and conservancy recently won kudos from the Rhode Island Natural History Survey, the organization commissioned to write the first ecological study of Napatree. The group was rehired to review management practices on the point. The resulting report is entirely laudatory and urges the conservancy and fire district to continue gathering data and educating visitors on Napatree's conservation value.[35]

PERHAPS IT IS FITTING that a seminal legal case concerning access to the Rhode Island shore grew out of a squabble in Westerly. In 1977, six members of the Rhode Island Mobile Sportfishermen association were arrested while cleaning up debris along several miles of beach. They were charged with trespassing on the oceanfront property of Wilfred Kay, in the Misquamicut section. Kay said the men were walking above the mean high-water line, which he had staked. That line was under water at the time. The fishermen believed they had the right to walk along the beach up to a more visible high-water mark, indicated by the seaweed left behind. "Let's get this into the courtroom," said the town's exasperated police chief, who had been caught in the middle of previous spats between the two sides.[36]

If the chief was hoping for a definitive guideline to settle future disputes, he was no doubt disappointed. The matter ultimately landed before the Rhode Island Supreme Court, whose decision did little to clarify the boundary between public trust land and private property. In *State v. Ibbison*, the court ruled that the official boundary is the mean high-tide line as "determined over a period of years using modern scientific techniques."[37] This put the cutoff seaward of the seaweed line, but where exactly it lay was still virtually unknowable to the average beachcomber. The court fully acknowledged the line's invisibility, asserting that if a town wished to charge someone with beach trespass in the future, authorities would have to prove beyond reasonable doubt that the trespasser knew where the boundary was and intentionally crossed it.

"The court essentially said it's unenforceable," says Robert Thompson, chair of the University of Rhode Island's department of marine affairs. (In his estimation, a more logical boundary, both historically and practically, is the "wrack" or seaweed line.)

Adding to the confusion, this elusive line in the sand also shifts from state to state and is constantly being redrawn by the courts. In Maine, one of the few states where oceanfront dwellers generally own the shore all the way to the low-tide line, its supreme court recently expanded public access slightly by granting scuba divers the right to cross the intertidal zone.[38] In Texas, on the other hand, the state supreme court has sharply curtailed public-access rights of late in favor of private property owners. In 2012, the court ruled that when a major storm, erosion, or sea-level rise pushes the public section of the beach back onto private property, the public's right to access that beach has been effectively washed away.[39]

According to a national survey of people involved in coastal-management issues, rising property values and vigorous residential construction are the primary culprits behind the increasing conflict over waterfront access. Changing demographics further fuel tensions. The people living on the coast now tend to be both wealthier and older than in the past, and they usually aren't relying on the ocean to make a living.[40] Tolerance for shared uses has gradually been displaced by worries about loss of privacy, property damage, and habitat degradation. Reconciling competing visions of life on the shore has become a never-ending task for state and local officials.

In the most coveted locales, beaches and waterfront once open for the wandering are carefully monitored and their access closely guarded. In Martha's Vineyard, regulations restrict the comings and goings of summer tourists to such a degree that some call it "beach apartheid."[41] Likewise, on Nantucket, the super-rich now so dominate the island that, in 2005, a *New York Times* article referred to it as "nature's ultimate gated community."[42]

Greenwich, Connecticut, was forced to open up its beaches to nonresidents after an out-of-town law student who was prevented from jogging through Greenwich Point Park fought the residents-only policy all the way to the state Supreme Court—and won. "It is remarkable how deeply angry Greenwich is about letting in people who aren't paying their high taxes," the jogger, Brenden Leydon, later told the *Los Angeles Times*.[43]

Thompson says that, having previously lived in California, where protecting shoreline access is a cause célèbre, he finds Rhode Islanders to be surprisingly nonchalant about their shore rights. People ought to be more vigilant, he says, and offers this analogy: New York's Central Park is a treasured resource that belongs to the public. Consider what would happen if 80 percent of visitors were restricted to a tiny portion of that park. People would think that grossly unfair. But that, Thompson says, is what's happening along the country's shoreline, due to lack of access, lack of parking, the loss of affordable seaside accommodations, and confusion about the law. "In a way," Thompson says, "we're creating a hierarchy of access. It's silent, and it's insidious."

In Rhode Island, the state Coastal Resources Management Council is charged with designating and marking public rights-of-way to the shore. The agency has been fairly aggressive in this regard, and it publishes a comprehensive guide to legal access points. But CRMC's own reports acknowledge that the lack of parking at access points hinders their use, while progress in opening up new pathways has been stymied by a lack of state funding for the program. The CRMC's stated goal is to designate at least one right-of-way for each mile of shoreline. But the agency has been stuck at just past the halfway mark, adding just five rights-of-way, to total 221, over the past decade.[44]

The Rhode Island Mobile Sportfishermen (RIMS), the group involved in the *Ibbison* case, continues to be a vociferous advocate for shore access, a right obviously vital to their interests. In particular, the organization has aggressively defended access to Quonochontaug ("Quonnie") Beach, in Westerly's very private and not very accessible Weekapaug section. Another undeveloped barrier beach, Quonnie shelters a saltwater pond to its north and is a popular spot for fishing and bird-watching. Much of the peninsula is owned by the Nope's Island Conservation Association, whose board of directors is made up of nearby property owners. Quonnie is also another protected plover area, under agreements signed with Fish and Wildlife.

A sand trail for vehicles runs the length of the beach, a distance of more than a mile. (The trail is open to the public in the off-season; during the summer months, non-landowners must walk in.) RIMS owns two lots at the eastern end of Quonnie, which its members use for fishing. But in order to reach one of the lots, members have to leave the sand trail and drive across ten to forty feet of Nope's territory.[45] Immediately after RIMS quietly bought that second lot in 1999, Nope's strongly objected to the vehicle crossings, citing damage to the beach. The dispute hit a new low in 2008 when ten nail-studded boards were found hidden in the trail.[46] After years of quarreling, RIMS took the matter to Superior Court. In 2011, a judge ruled in the fishermen's favor.

The court found that the family that previously owned the lot had routinely crossed the land now owned by Nope's in order to use their property for fishing, quahogging, duck hunting, and the occasional clambake. That historical access, by foot and vehicle, the judge concluded, entitles RIMS to continue crossing Nope's territory, even if its members' use is more intensive than in the past. The alternatives—ferrying members in by boat or walking the length of the trail with fishing gear—are not only "a major inconvenience," the judge concluded, but "strikingly different" from what the previous owners had done for nearly a century.[47]

As for damage to the beach, in the opinion of the court, Nope's failed to prove any significant environmental harm.

But the fight goes on. Nope's has appealed the decision to the state supreme court.

TOWN AUTHORITIES IN WESTERLY must walk a fine line between advocating for public access to the shoreline and respecting the rights of private-property owners. When it comes to Napatree, officials are supportive of the Watch Hill groups' conservation efforts in the sense that "it's not something the taxpayers have to pay for," says Hartford, the town manager. However, concerns about constraints on public access were compelling enough in 2008 that the Town Council began looking into whether Fort Road, a now-nebulous roadway originally used to reach the cottages on the point, might be declared public. A lawyer for the fire district and conservancy responded with the threat of a "long and expensive" lawsuit.[48] Ultimately, the council backed off and instead passed a symbolic resolution affirming the public's right to pass onto Napatree in perpetuity. "We reached kind of a détente with the conservancy and the fire district," says Hartford. "But we'll defend the public's right to access out there. And they know that."

Meanwhile, another turf war is brewing, this time over control of the town's harbors and, more specifically, its mooring fields. Coastal towns in Rhode Island are required to institute formal plans for managing their harbors, but the commission charged with that task in Westerly has been stalled by conflict, turnover, and lack of will for nearly a decade. (Saunders is one of the more consistent members, having served on the volunteer board for six years.) The people and entities that currently hold sway over mooring distribution in town are not eager to give up that control in favor of what the state says should be an "orderly, safe, equitable and efficient" allocation of harbor space.[49]

Moorings (the anchored lines used to secure a vessel) have been a flashpoint since the late 1980s, when they became a popular alternative to increasingly expensive boat slips. "We saw the proliferation of moorings going out willy-nilly in the state's waters," says Jeff Willis, the deputy director of the CRMC, which oversees the harbor-management process. "Towns had de facto management systems in place through marinas and yacht clubs."

Such is the case in Westerly, where there has been "sort of a vacuum of town oversight" over mooring fields, acknowledges Hartford. In some cases, the town left it to fire districts and yacht clubs to handle the distribution of public moorings and only stepped in to settle major disputes. Now, members of those clubs dominate those fields. "One way to look at it is they've tried to take control," Hartford says. "Another is they've tried to maintain order."

Watch Hill Harbor has an order of its own. Saunders came to that conclusion after he applied for a mooring in the public field around the private yacht club. He was told that he would be notified when his name reached the top of the list and a suitable mooring became available. Fifteen years went by before Saunders finally demanded to see the list himself. There was his name at the top. He also inspected the list of people who already had moorings. People who put their names on the waiting list years after he had, Saunders says, had managed to jump the line and secure a mooring well ahead of him. How? He can only speculate, but an earlier state study on how to manage Little Narragansett Bay noted that moorings in Watch Hill cove are usually "handed down" among yacht club members or "given over to the yacht club."[50] A 2010 letter to mooring holders from a club official suggested that some mooring holders also rent out, rather than give up, their unused moorings.[51]

Because the yacht club is located in a federal navigation project, its domination of the mooring field is in direct conflict with US Army Corps of Engineers rules, according to Willis. The Army Corps requires that a federal project being used as a mooring field be open to all on equal terms. "When you have a situation like the one in Watch Hill where a private entity is controlling the moorings, the Army Corps of Engineers isn't happy with that," Willis says. "So now the town has to figure out how to run it according to Army Corps standards.

"As much as the yacht club doesn't want to hear that," he adds, "that's what they're going to have to do."

Ultimately, the CRMC and the town will have to sign off on the plan for how the mooring field is managed. Watch Hill's proposed solution is to let them handle it themselves. Early in 2012, the fire district was pushing the town's harbor commission for authority to name its own assistant harbormaster, who, under the harbor-management plan, would have the same power as the town harbormaster to oversee Watch Hill Harbor and Little Narragansett Bay.

Also in 2012, as the harbor commission continued its deliberations on the management plan, Barnes and Simmons let it be known that they'd run out of patience with the naysayers questioning their actions on Napatree. In a letter to the commission's chairman, the men claimed that their conservation measures had been falsely attacked as covert efforts to shut down Napatree and that those attacks had made it into the commission's record. They cited no specifics and mentioned no names. They only issued what sounded like a warning, saying it is time "for the slanders and libels to stop."[52]

If the strongly worded letter was meant to silence critics, it seemed to have had the opposite effect. Saunders saw to it that the letter made its way into the local newspaper. And its publication elicited a response from Don Morris, one of the fishermen arrested on the trespassing charges that led to the *Ibbison* ruling.[53] Three decades later, Morris said in his letter that shore access in Rhode Island hasn't improved—it's been severely diminished by "well-heeled organizations and property owners" and that "the public's rights to the shore are just as misunderstood as they were before the decision." In his own shore outings, Morris wrote, he finds himself reenacting the 1977 beach confrontation over and over again: "Just this morning, I was confronted by a property owner who has blocked public access and then threatened me with a police call."

A few months later, in September 2012, Morris's point was brought home by a highly publicized lawsuit. The Rhode Island attorney general's office had filed suit against seven beachfront property owners in the town's Misquamicut section, claiming that the homeowners were illegally blocking public access along a two-mile stretch of sand. In this case, the exact location of the mean high-tide line was not the issue. These property owners had put up no-trespassing signs and fences on sand that the attorney general says clearly never belonged to them. The state's evidence is a 1909 map showing the original subdivision that included these properties. The house lots only extend to the base of the dunes, the attorney general's office charges. The rest of the beach, roughly eighty feet between the dunes and the water, had been dedicated to the public.[54]

FIVE

Priority Population: Darien, Connecticut

THE APTLY NAMED NEARWATER Lane, in the Connecticut shoreline suburb of Darien, is the sole route home for those Wall Street titans, corporate executives, and heirs to privilege who inhabit a peninsula known as Noroton Neck. Breaking away from the commercial congestion of the Boston Post Road, Nearwater makes a beeline through the verdant cape, passing beneath old-growth shade trees and along deep front lawns, past the closely clustered homes of a private beach community, past the entrance to the town beach, and finally halting at the waterfront estates that claim the peninsula's furthest tip on Long Island Sound. The lane is the only access way onto the Neck, whose curved appendages protect enough coves and inlets to make the area a haven for sailing enthusiasts. Developers spotted its potential as early as the 1920s, when Thomas Crimmins, the son of prosperous Irish immigrants, began carving a portion of the peninsula into building lots.

After dredging the harbor on the east shore to create a yacht basin, Crimmins's company built a pier on the west shore, subdivided the land, and designated a private beach for the exclusive use of property owners.[1] According to an easement laying out the extent of those beach rights in 1931, "bona fide" guests of the property owner were welcome but with some exceptions: beach privileges were never to be extended to "any person or persons of the Hebrew race."[2] For several decades thereafter, Darien would come to be known as a community almost wholly reserved for white Protestants. Sociologist and author James W. Loewen has gone so far as to label Darien a "sundown town," the term for towns that actively kept out African Americans and other groups in the interest of remaining "all white."[3]

If anti-Semitism no longer distinguishes Noroton Neck, it is still, like much of Darien, a province of privilege. And members-only socializing remains a hallmark of Darien life. The town of twenty thousand has no fewer than eight private clubs, including three country clubs and a hunt club. At the top of the social pecking order is the highly selective Wee Burn, an old-line golf club where debutantes were once feted at fancy cotillions and female club members were still fighting for full club privileges as recently as 1997.[4] Darien has its own barriers to entry. Single-family homes sell for an average of $1.6 million.[5] Starter homes—in the $600,000s—are generally found in densely developed Noroton Heights, which once housed the European immigrants who serviced the old estates along Darien's coast. Prices rise precipitously the closer one gets to the coveted shore communities, which, in addition to Noroton Neck, include Long Neck Point, Contentment Island, and Tokeneke. These are aspiration addresses, locations that telegraph status.[6] On Nearwater Lane, in 2010, a six-thousand-square-foot colonial with a three-car garage and in-ground pool on two acres fetched nearly $5 million for its then-owner, Richard C. Breeden, the former Securities and Exchange Commission chairman.[7]

Buyers here commonly pay multiple millions for homes they fully intend to tear down and replace with something grander. They aren't just paying for the bucolic landscape and water views—figuring heavily into their investment calculus are also privacy, security, and resale value. What they ultimately want, however, is something without a definitive price tag. As the residents of Nearwater Lane were reminded a few years back, no matter how much you shell out, it's never enough to buy certainty.

It was Christopher and Margaret Stefanoni who upset the social order after moving to 77 Nearwater Lane in 1999. A couple of brainy Harvard grads, they came from starkly different backgrounds: he, a scrappy athlete raised by a struggling single mom in Massachusetts; she, a quiet, self-described nerd who grew up in Guatemala, where her Harvard-educated parents ran a coffee business. According to Chris, they found each other in Cambridge, grew close while working together on real estate deals, and wound up eloping. When Chris decided to put his MBA to use in a finance career, the couple decided to move closer to New York City.

In some respects, Darien was a natural landing place. The train commute into the city was a tolerable forty-five minutes. The town's sixteen miles of coastline appealed to Chris, an avid swimmer. The couple's young son could attend the excellent public schools (as would his four siblings to come). And Margaret, who goes by Peggy, had strong family ties to the town; as a child, she'd often visited Darien to see her grandfather, who was chief of clinical chemotherapy at the Sloan-Kettering Cancer Center.

If Darien seemed right for the Stefanonis in theory, in practice, the Stefanonis were not at all, and nor did they aspire to be, the Darien type. Perhaps Chris harbored resentment toward the rich from a childhood spent in want. Perhaps Peggy was put off by Darien's homogeneity compared to life in Guatemala. Whatever the reasons, the Stefanonis placed little value on fitting in. They weren't interested in club memberships. They did not take exotic vacations or dine at fancy restaurants. And they eschewed the kind of luxuries that advertised wealth. Happy with thrift-shop finds, Chris tended toward Dickies, Peggy toward loose-fitting sweaters. Instead of Range Rovers and BMWs, they drove a well-worn minivan and a vintage Volvo. They were certainly sharp enough to know how the social climbing game was played—while at Harvard, Chris had made his way into one of the exclusive male final clubs. But they derived far more satisfaction from bucking the norms than hewing to them.

This attitude of nonconformity extended to their approach to real estate investment. While living in Massachusetts, they had practiced ferreting out undervalued properties and removing encumbrances to make them buildable, mainly in affluent areas. Chris's rule of thumb was that the best deals are the ones no one else wants. In Darien, 77 Nearwater seemed to meet that litmus test. A dated contemporary, it was nothing special—any other buyer would have probably torn it down and built anew. The draw for the Stefanonis was the one-acre lot and its location next to a large tidewater pool known as Holly Pond. Although the property didn't include frontage on the pond, an easement across a neighboring property to the back guaranteed access to the water. Trees blocked the view from the house, but trees weren't permanent. The Stefanonis saw potential and snatched up the property for $800,000.

They hadn't been there long before they hired contractors to clear away trees and vegetation. Relations with the neighbors quickly soured, especially since the cutting strayed over property lines. The town insisted that the Stefanonis restore some of the plantings, which were within a regulated coastal zone.[8] Tensions eased temporarily, until another point of contention arose: the Stefanonis began to zealously pursue dock rights on the pond, a privilege their neighbor believed was rightfully his. The discord worsened, and the battle over easement rights moved from their backyards into the courts.

Even as the legal battle played out, however, the Stefanonis hit upon another way of upping the value of their property. This approach didn't demand compliance with so many expectations and regulations, and would perhaps even accomplish a public good: in compliance with Sec. 8-30g of the state laws, the Stefanonis had decided to tear down their house and replace it with an affordable-housing development.[9]

If the Stefanonis' proposal made a mockery of the surrounding neighborhood's exclusivity, under the law, it was also very viable. When the plan was announced, the neighborhood reaction was absolutely apoplectic. "People were violent," recalls Evonne Klein, the first selectman at the time. "I had a guy put his fist in my face: 'You haven't done anything about this. You need to *do* something about it!'"

MUCH LIKE 40B, THE MASSACHUSETTS law, 8-30g acts as a fairly strong foot in the door of communities historically closed to affordable housing.[10] Adopted in 1989, and amended since, it simply requires that communities rejecting an affordable-housing project come up with some solid reasons why. If a developer appeals such a rejection in court, the town bears the burden of proof to show that the project's impact would be so detrimental to the public interest (i.e., health and safety) it would do more harm than good.[11] It is not enough to turn away below-market-rate housing because it conflicts with zoning, threatens town "character," or might add children to the public schools. The rationale more likely to pass muster with the courts would be an inadequate water supply or insufficient sewage facilities.[12] Wetlands protections also apply.

Towns are shielded from 8-30g once 10 percent or more of their housing stock meets the state's definition of affordable.[13] But Darien, like all of the high-priced suburbs around it, falls far short of that threshold. In 2005, when the Stefanonis began designing their development, Darien's affordable-housing count added up to just 1.8 percent. Further weakening the town's position was its long neglect of the issue. The last time Darien officials had sought to build affordable housing on their own terms was 1989, the year

8-30g went through. The proposal then, for thirty condominiums, so outraged some residents that they fought it, unsuccessfully, all the way to the US Court of Appeals.[14] Finally completed in 1994, the project, Clock Hill Homes, was the town's last attempt to actively encourage such housing.

The Stefanonis' plan called for twenty condominiums in two structures designed to resemble a manor house and barn. Six of the condos would be offered at below-market rates of $160,000 to $220,000. The project was to be strictly for seniors, and the need for such housing was undeniable. The Clock Hill condos always had a waiting list of buyers, and renters were lined up sixty deep for the rare opening at the town's thirty-unit elderly-housing complex.[15]

But angry Noroton Neck residents didn't want any high-density housing on Nearwater Lane. They saw the project as not just a threat to the single-family sanctity of their own neighborhood but to the town as a whole. "We do not want to set precedence [*sic*] for other areas in town if this goes down so easily," warned an e-mail circulated by opponents.

The Stefanonis' immediate neighbors fumed that the affordable-housing plan was a form of retaliation for their objections to the land-clearing and claim to dock rights, a charge the couple has consistently denied.[16] Regardless, their plan had struck a more central nerve in town, evidenced by the turnout for the planning and zoning commission's first public hearing on the matter. Although it was a weeknight, several hundred people packed the town hall auditorium. Chris Stefanoni had alerted local media about the hearing, and their presence only added to residents' ire. One man cursed at a television cameraman, suggesting he go cover something else.[17] When the Stefanonis began their presentation, the crowd hissed and snickered, eventually prompting a scolding from the commission chairman.

That evening was the beginning of an extended stretch of mutual vituperations. The Stefanonis were not cowed by the rudeness and open resentment, an outpouring that would continue well beyond that evening. Far from intimidated by the town's wealth, the Stefanonis would deflect accusations of greed hurled their way by seizing on Darien's pervasive privilege as evidence of the need for housing diversity. Darien was too sheltered and overwhelmingly white, they crowed, pointing to the high school parents' association's pitch for a "slave auction" as a possible theme for that year's post-prom party.[18] Chris Stefanoni publicly reveled in the notion of an 8-30g housing complex nestled in among the rich and powerful. "It would be a lot easier to just build a McMansion, sell, and move to another town," he told me at the time. "But Darien has enough McMansions. Darien needs some humility."[19]

The Stefanonis were uniquely suited for this fight. They lived like paupers in a sparsely furnished house, managed to do their own legal work, and avoided debt. (The only status that has ever seemed to concern them is the athletic standing of their children.) And they were extraordinarily persistent. In short, they had staying power, so much so that the battle over 77 Nearwater dragged on for a full two years. Chris had abandoned the notion of a job on Wall Street; he focused all his attention on the housing fight. When the dust finally cleared, the condo project was off the table—but the Stefanonis were millionaires. An anonymous donor or donors had effectively bought them out. Delivered in the form of a grant from the New York Community Trust to the Darien Land Trust, the money enabled the land trust to acquire the property.[20] The Stefanonis' price: $4.2 million.

Chris says that he and Peggy took the deal because it beat the alternative—opponents of their proposed affordable-housing project appeared ready and willing to keep the Stefanonis' development plan tied up in the courts for years. The price reflected the property's new development value—and, for the anonymous donor(s) perhaps, the cost of future certainty. Today, 77 Nearwater is a lovely wildflower meadow.

Was this the Stefanonis' plan all along? Was their 8-30g application a ruse, a high-stakes game of chicken? Many people in Darien thought so, especially after the couple began to buy up more property in town. They have since filed three more 8-30g applications, all for senior housing. Some call the Stefanonis extortionists; a local lawyer who went to Hartford to rail against the affordable-housing law before a legislative panel took it a step further and, without mentioning any names, declared that, in Darien, 8-30g had become a tool for "economic terrorism."[21]

Chris acknowledges that his motives for pursuing affordable housing are not pure—"I'm not altruistic." But he doesn't see himself as any worse than the rest of the diehard capitalists who live in town—and perhaps a little better. "I'm not like the guys on Wall Street who are gambling with other people's money," he says. He and Peggy simply found a niche: Darien's long inaction on affordable housing. And if financial gain is one aim, they also firmly believe that Darien is long overdue for the economic and racial diversity such housing could bring.

In effect, they have become Darien's worst nightmare: canny crusaders who are persistent, vocal, and unconcerned with status. They are opportunists waving the banner of social justice, attention-getters in a town that prefers to conduct business unnoticed.

They are not what the drafters of 8-30g had in mind, and rare is the developer who could or would exist as the Stefanonis do: in a constant state of legal warfare. As Chris himself says, "You gotta be a little bit nuts to do this." But if the Stefanonis are extreme, their unflagging presence has also forced Darien to have the necessary conversation it did not want to have. And, in this way, 8-30g has served its purpose. Darien has had to confront the reality that if the town does not plan for and generate more affordable housing on its own terms, then the Stefanonis might do it for them.

• • •

MORE THAN HALF A century has passed since the release of the film *Auntie Mame,* in which the exuberant, free-spirited Mame, played by Rosalind Russell, refuses to allow her beloved nephew to be molded into a stuffy elitist. Specifically, Mame does not want the young man to wind up like his soon-to-be-ex girlfriend, whom she refers to as an "Aryan from Darien."[22] Mame's notorious slam of Darien followed an earlier and equally unflattering film portrayal of the town as close-minded and intolerant. *Gentleman's Agreement,* starring Gregory Peck, referenced what was said to be an informal understanding among Darien property owners that no one would sell real estate to Jews.[23]

The big-screen depictions of Darien weren't based on hearsay. Darien was known to be a "restricted" community, which was a fairly common phenomenon outside many major cities by the 1920s.[24] Developers had figured out that promises of exclusivity drew buyers. Real estate advertisements freely used the term "restricted" as a selling point. An advertisement in the *New York Times* for a property for sale in South Norwalk, Connecticut, described a "Highly restricted desirable home at Harbor View Beach." Another ad, for a Connecticut beach house overlooking a golf course, omitted the exact location but specified instead that it was a "restricted section."[25] The ads did not spell out the restrictions, but the implication was clear: the neighborhoods were "safe" for a certain class and color of people. Developers often spelled out the restrictions in covenants written into the property deeds. Early on, the covenants restricted the kinds of uses allowed on the property and set design and cost standards. Over time, however, restrictions were extended to exclude certain types of people, like the ban on Jews at the Noroton Neck beach.

After the term "restricted" went out of favor, Darien continued to uphold the sentiment. Loewen tells of a sign that was posted on Darien's Hollow Tree Ridge Road during the 1940s that openly designated the area for "Gentiles Only."[26] As time went on, intolerance was broadcast in other ways. In the 1950s, for example, when an all-black church from Harlem expressed interest in buying a twenty-one-room Darien estate for use as a summer camp, the town quickly adopted zoning rules that made such a use impossible.[27] In 1960, a Yale student reported that anti-Catholic pamphlets were being distributed at Darien's Republican headquarters.[28]

In 1965, Darien's superintendent of schools, Gregory Coffin, decided the homogeneous climate was harmful because kids in town were too removed from the real world. As documented in the online archives of the Martin Luther King Jr. Center for Nonviolent Social Change, Coffin wrote to King to tell of his plan to unite church youth groups from all-white Darien and racially diverse Stamford to watch a video tape of one of King's speeches.[29] King, according to a handwritten draft of his response, expressed hope that Coffin would be successful at "breaking down the walls" in Darien.[30] But a year later, when Coffin left Darien for a new job, he worried aloud that the community's hypersegregated atmosphere was still "most unhealthy."

"It's the artificiality of the racial thing that I'm worried about," Coffin said, "that because of their money and position, these kids will probably be leaders, and they're being prepared for that role with only a wildly unrealistic view of life." He joked darkly that he'd sold his home in town to a white Christian "because I didn't think quickly enough to get around the realtors' 'Gentleman's Agreement.'"[31]

All these decades later, one would think that Darien's once-notorious reputation would have faded. By now, the line from *Auntie Mame* might have worn into a distasteful cliché, and those early displays of prejudice written off as "of an era." And yet, if you plug "Aryan from Darien" into the Google search engine, the term still turns up in discussions about the town with surprising frequency. One commenter advises someone pondering a move to Darien: "I was married to an 'Aryan from Darien'; she just couldn't shake it off. I wouldn't do that to my kids."[32] And in another parenting discussion: "The famous line 'The Aryan from Darien' is still true, according to an Arab woman I sat next to on the plane. She's found living there with her baby difficult; ethnic homogeneity & conformity are the norm, she says."[33]

The truth is, Darien has never quite shed its pre-civil-rights-era reputation for intolerance. Certainly its demographics, which haven't changed much since Coffin's day, don't do much to dispel the image.[34] Even though the town is flanked by the very diverse cities of Norwalk and Stamford to its east and west, respectively, Darien remains the "whitest" suburb along Connecticut's Gold Coast and, as of 2010, the wealthiest, with a median household income of $185,619.[35]

How is it that Darien has remained so white and so extremely wealthy for decades? The usual answer to the question of homogeneous demographic makeup is that there is a natural sorting effect. Expensive, attractive suburbs draw highly educated, affluent people who demand high-performing schools and safe surroundings for their children. Though this is legitimate on the face of it, natural selection does not tell the whole story of the town's homogeneity. History also has a lasting impact on the shape and tone of exclusive suburbs such as Darien. The homeowners of today who zealously guard their two-acre zoning are, whether they know it or not, perpetuating a pattern of exclusion laid down long ago.

In Darien, "gentleman's agreements" and restrictive covenants set a tone later enforced by strict zoning. Darien was an early adopter of zoning, putting its first rules in place in 1925. The restrictions gradually became more stringent, and in the 1950s, the town banned apartment buildings. Incredibly, for such a rapidly developing metro area, that prohibition would endure into the 1980s.[36] The thinking behind the apartment ban was boldly expressed in Darien's town plan: "It is not necessary for the town to provide, nor does it intend to provide, all of the possible types of residential environments."[37]

That same decade, under increasing pressure to lift its ban on multifamily housing, Darien hired a consultant to defend its exclusivity. The consultant proclaimed Darien a valuable haven, one "attractive for the upper-management people who work and employ less-skilled and less-mobile labor."[38] If deprived of a place like Darien, in which they can feel comfortable, the employers might leave the area altogether, the consultant warned. The implied assumption was that upper-income people would not feel comfortable in a town with a broader range of housing and classes. Loewen is more blunt in his assessment of Darien's special appeal to the upper classes: "One reason Darien's residents choose Darien is because living there tells the world that one has the money and social power to avoid African Americans and other people of lower social status."[39]

The needs of its own elderly population finally caused the town to lift its ban on apartments in 1983. A decade passed before a major developer, AvalonBay Communities, turned up. Avalon wanted to build a 189-unit development on thirty-two acres near the train station. A quarter of the apartments were to be affordable. The town's response was hardly welcoming: saying they wanted the land for town amenities, officials took steps to repel the project by condemning the property. Voters ultimately derailed that strategy, however—they could not stomach the $27 million buyout price.[40] Avalon built its project.

Today, whether homebuyers choose Darien for the waterfront, the school system, or the "people like us" factor, the town's exclusivity cannot be solely attributed to individual preferences or the workings of the free market. History shows that Darien has actively cultivated and defended exclusivity as its "brand" for decades.

Certainly present-day Darien is not the bigoted place ridiculed in *Auntie Mame*. Since 1981, the community has hosted a chapter of A Better Chance, which sponsors six inner-city students so they may attend Darien High School. The Avalon apartments were recently publicly praised by a top town official as "the best thing that's happened to our town."[41] And in recent years, spurred by the Stefanonis and 8-30g pressures, a few people in town have worked tirelessly to build support for affordable housing. Notably, the Darien Housing Authority, after a years-long effort, has finally obtained financing and town approvals to redevelop and expand its tired rental housing, which dates to the 1950s.

"Most people living here now were born after *Gentleman's Agreement* came out and don't even know about it," says Evonne Klein, the former first selectman, who, it's worth noting, was elected to her post with a Jewish name (her husband's). "I don't think the new generation is thinking that way."

Still, Klein has acknowledged that as late as the 1990s, when she ran for the town's board of education, she was advised to run under her maiden name, Gallucci, and she did—just that once.[42] Even now, there are people in town, some in positions of power, who remain firmly committed to what Klein calls "protecting the brand." The "unfortunate thing," she goes on, is "when you have people who think a certain way and then they make proclamations in public, it doesn't allow communities like Darien to shed the *Gentleman's Agreement* reputation."

WHILE SHE WAS THE first selectman, from 2003 to 2009, Klein pushed for action on affordable housing, partly because she had to: homeowners were demanding she do something to fend off the Stefanonis. One relatively easy change she supported was "inclusionary" zoning. Inclusionary zoning is common practice in the cities of Norwalk and Stamford, where it is seen as a painless way of continually adding to the stock of affordable housing. The policy is fairly simple: it mandates that all new market-rate developments must include a set percentage of affordable units.[43]

Darien's planning and zoning commission, under the watchful eye of chairman Frederick B. Conze, was not inclined to go along.

A veteran member of the elected commission, Conze wasn't a fan of affordable housing generally. He had once declared at a public hearing (to enthusiastic applause) that the problem with affordable housing is that "the people who are the neighbors around the project, they're the ones who have to take the bullet." He went on: "I have to honestly tell you that I look at this as a virus. That once you open this box, you never get it back into the bottle, because it will be replicated all the way around town."[44]

Nevertheless, in 2009, with the specter of Chris Stefanoni hanging about and after protracted debate, Conze and the commission signed off on a modest inclusionary strategy. The regulation they approved requires at least 12 percent of the units in new multifamily projects and subdivisions to be reserved for people earning no more than 80 percent of the state median income.[45] In truth, the policy is unlikely to generate much affordable housing—because Darien is nearly built out, big projects are few and far between.[46] Still, Darien's approval of the policy seemed to mark a milestone for a town that hadn't been proactive on the issue. A state housing organization said Darien deserved "five gold stars."[47]

What went largely unnoticed until several months later was that Darien's "inclusionary" policy was actually kind of exclusionary. According to the language worked out by the zoning commission and town counsel, new affordable units were to be offered to a designated "Priority Population." People who had dibs were listed in order of priority:

1. Darien residents who volunteer as first responders
2. Darien public employees
3. Darien residents who work in town
4. Darien residents
5. Nonresidents who work in Darien
6. Former residents who want to move back
7. All others

The list wasn't unusual in the sense that policies granting housing preference to residents and town workers are fairly common. Towns understandably want to take care of people with ties to their community. Indeed, the need in their own backyards is often what prompts towns to pursue affordable housing on their own.

Residency preferences for workforce housing are not illegal, but at the same time, the preferences cannot be used as a way to keep out certain groups. The Fair Housing Act prohibits housing discrimination on the basis of a range of protected categories, including race, color, and national origin. And the US Department of Housing and Urban Development (HUD), as well as state housing-finance offices, has strict guidelines for the fair marketing of affordable housing to a range of potential applicants. Local preferences are typically allowed as long as they are implemented in a way that doesn't have a greater impact on minorities.[48]

Darien's preference rankings were unusually lengthy. People from outside Darien were at the back of a very long line, a line in which even *former* Darien residents were allowed to cut in front. When asked for their perspective on the preferences, fair-housing experts suggested that, if not discriminatory in its wording, Darien's policy held the potential to be discriminatory in practice. Diane Houk, then the executive director of the Fair Housing Justice Center in New York, told me for a story for the *New York Times* that she found the preferences to be "highly suspect" in a town that was 94 percent white. "If I were the town," she said, "I would want to have an assessment done on what the impact will be."[49]

Darien officials seemed unconcerned—the preferences stayed in place. But about six months after the *Times* story, in May 2010, Darien's newly elected first selectman, David Campbell, received a letter from the Civil Rights Division of the US Department of Justice. The department was opening an investigation into whether Darien's zoning and land-use practices violated the Fair Housing

Act. More specifically, investigators wanted to know why the town had adopted the "Priority Population" clause.[50]

This was a particularly sensitive issue at the time. Just to the north, similarly white enclaves in Westchester County, New York, were the target of a lawsuit claiming they took HUD dollars without complying with fair-housing mandates. In 2009, a federal judge ruled that the county had "utterly failed" to meet its fair-housing obligations, and the county now faced a mandate to build 750 units of affordable housing in predominantly white communities.[51]

Campbell kept the investigation quiet. Word only got out after DOJ investigators contacted the Stefanonis (who were happy to share information about the town's reaction to their affordable-housing plans). Conze, who works in real estate, repeatedly denied any discriminatory intent behind the preferences. "The intentions by passing this were completely genuine, and were focused on a very specific need," he said, referring to the housing-cost burden on existing residents, "and were not designed to be exclusionary but rather to address that specific need."[52] After meeting with DOJ investigators, however, Conze voted along with the rest of his commission to repeal the controversial language. In its place, a new requirement specifies that all affordable units "be offered for sale or rent in compliance with all applicable federal and state Fair Housing laws."

The amendment put the issue to rest. But the DOJ was now interested enough in Darien to keep its investigation open.

THE HINDLEY ELEMENTARY SCHOOL, at the head of Nearwater Lane, is, like the other public schools in Darien, a neighborhood school that wants for little. Students here are way ahead of the average Connecticut kid academically—in 2011, about half of all third graders at Hindley scored at the advanced level in mathematics on the Connecticut Mastery Test. Less than 5 percent failed to show proficiency.[53]

Just two miles away, across the border in the city of Stamford, is an elementary school of roughly the same size called K. T. Murphy. Although the students attending school here live within minutes of Darien, their circumstances are dramatically different. Nearly half of all students at K. T. Murphy are eligible for free or reduced-price meals; not a single student at Hindley falls into this category. A third of K. T. Murphy students are not fluent in English. And when it comes to academic performance, K. T. Murphy students have made progress in recent years but are still well behind those at Hindley: about 20 percent of Murphy third graders missed the proficiency mark in math in 2011.[54]

Leaving Hindley but headed in the other direction, toward the city of Norwalk, a four-mile drive brings you to Brookside Elementary. Students here have much more in common with the Stamford kids than they do with their geographically closer peers at Hindley. Like K. T. Murphy's, about 75 percent of Brookside's school population is from a minority group. And, as at K. T. Murphy, about half are eligible for subsidized meals. Brookside is highly regarded for its success with English-language learners and disadvantaged students, but still, when it comes to math, a quarter of third graders lacked proficiency in 2011.[55]

Three elementary schools within a six-mile radius but deeply segregated by race, by income, and by achievement—such stark contrasts between bordering communities are the norm along Connecticut's southwestern coast. In fact, Darien sits smack dab in the middle of what one researcher has concluded is the most inequitably divided metro area *in the entire country*. Why? At least part of the answer has to do with restrictive zoning.

Jonathan Rothwell, a senior research analyst and associate fellow at the Brookings Institution, conducted a detailed analysis of a hundred metro areas in the United States, comparing the degree of segregation within each by income, housing costs, and academic achievement.[56] Six of the ten metro areas with the largest disparity in test scores between low-income students and other students are in the Northeast. Three are in Connecticut: the Bridgeport-Stamford-Norwalk metro area; the New Haven area; and the Hartford-West Hartford-East Hartford area. The areas most divided by achievement are also markedly segregated by income. Low-income students are heavily concentrated in lower-performing schools. And, as any parent who has tried to buy a home in a good school district in these areas well knows, it is far more expensive to live near a high-scoring school than a low-scoring school. In the Bridgeport metro area, in which Darien is located, Rothwell calculated that it is 3.5 times more expensive to live near a high-scoring school.

Though these findings aren't terribly surprising, Rothwell dug deeper to look at how restrictive the zoning is in the most deeply divided metro areas. He found that zoning is significantly more restrictive—meaning, it discourages or prevents the development of higher-density, lower-cost housing—in metro areas where the gaps between high-scoring and low-scoring districts are greatest, and where housing in good school districts is most expensive relative to marginal districts. In other words, school test-score gaps, housing-cost gaps, and restrictive zoning all seem to correlate.

Rothwell's conclusion: restrictive zoning is sharply limiting the supply of affordable housing, which bars poor children from high-quality schools and helps perpetuate deepening social inequities. "Just as explicitly race-based policies like covenants and discriminatory lending and real estate standards contravened market forces to keep blacks out of white neighborhoods," Rothwell writes, "zoning today keeps poor people out of rich neighborhoods, and accounts for a significant portion of the school test-score gap between low-income and other children."[57]

Advocates for strict zoning might say that Rothwell's findings demonstrate how effective zoning can be for bolstering property values. In Darien, for example, Conze, chairman of the planning and zoning commission, has made it clear that keeping home values high is the commission's main priority: "In effect, as elected officials, the commission is an organization tasked with managing . . . a diverse portfolio of real estate assets on behalf of 6,500 investors—representing the 6,500 home and property owners in Darien."[58]

But Rothwell and others argue that, by walling out less-advantaged kids, highly restrictive zoning is limiting economic opportunity and hobbling national economic gains. School-choice vouchers and charter schools are all well and good, they say, but these approaches alone aren't enough. Housing choice must also play a role in improving educational achievement, says Erin Boggs, the deputy director of the Connecticut Fair Housing Center.

"Right now we're in this Darwinian situation where the way you win the game is by keeping out low-income people," Boggs says. "That's the mindset of many towns in Connecticut. But our future is diversity—that is the population that is growing in Connecticut. By 2020, 27 percent of the working population here will be people of color.

"One way to deal with this situation is to put lots more resources into cities," she went on to say. "But that's only half of the equation. The other half is allowing people the choice to live in higher-opportunity areas."

Darien has tacitly acknowledged as much with its sponsorship of the A Better Chance program, which enables six inner-city students to temporarily live in town so they may attend the high school. Improving access to high-opportunity areas is also one rationale behind inclusionary zoning. New research shows that, when enthusiastically applied, inclusionary zoning can boost the academic achievement of low-income kids. A report from the Century Foundation found that an aggressive inclusionary zoning program in Montgomery County, Maryland, an affluent suburb of Washington, DC, has led to dramatic gains in school performance among low-income students there. The benefits were greatest when the low-income kids were in schools in which less than 20 percent of students qualified for free/reduced-price meals.[59]

Darien has opened its doors a crack wider of late by approving the Darien Housing Authority's expansion plans for the outdated public-housing complex. And, after the DOJ began poking around, Conze's commission green-lighted a private developer's plan to convert a vacant downtown office building into thirty-five small apartments, eleven of them affordable.

But town officials also pursued a parallel track, one that would relieve the pressure to be more inclusive by getting them out from under 8-30g—and the Stefanonis. In 2010, the Campbell administration scored a major coup when it persuaded the state to grant Darien a four-year moratorium from the affordable-housing law.

The wealthiest community in the state, a community that hadn't added any significant affordable housing since the Avalon apartments, and was the subject of an ongoing housing investigation by federal authorities, suddenly became the third town in all of Connecticut to win a reprieve from 8-30g.

AT THE TOP OF a narrow staircase, off a hallway crammed with kids' sports gear, is what the Stefanonis call their "war room." A small room lined with white wainscoting, it is bereft of décor. Two old desks face opposite walls—one for Chris, one for Peggy. Peggy's is stacked high with files, as is much of the area surrounding her desk. Folders peeking out from boxes beneath are labeled "Slave Auction" and "Anti-Semitism." Chris's desk, on the other hand, is almost clean, save for several lists written in tiny script.

This is 149 Nearwater, about a half-mile up the road from the site of the Stefanonis' first home, now the wildflower meadow. Some property owners have resisted selling to the Stefanonis, so in order to get this well-worn antique cape, the couple sent in Chris's mother (now deceased) as a straw buyer. Outside, a stone wall runs along one edge of their 1.5-acre property, coming to an abrupt halt as it nears the driveway. Unused stones and pallets are strewn about the yard. Chris hired guys to build the wall but stopped when the town hassled him about it being too high in places. The same goes for the yard—he's stopped mowing the lawn regularly. "This house looks like something in Appalachia," Chris says gleefully. "Everything that blows in my yard, I leave it there. This is my protest."

Darien, he says, has too many "bullies" who are used to getting whatever they want. He and Peggy are determined to give them a run for their money. Not surprisingly, they've made a few enemies in the process. After a local news affiliate interviewed them, a baseball dad they'd been friendly with e-mailed to say: "YOU BOTH SHOULD BE ASHAMED OF YOURSELVES OVER YOUR GREED, AND THAT IS WHAT IT IS ALL ABOUT. DO NOT EVER TALK TO ME AGAIN." They routinely receive magazine subscriptions they never ordered. At their old address, their mailbox was bashed off its post. They had to call the police to deal with a neighbor who repeatedly honked his horn every time he drove by their house.[60]

None of this dissuades them. It only bolsters their belief that they are the good guys in this fight. They are in perpetual litigation. Peggy spends so much time at a nearby law library that she has identified a "lucky desk." They spent three years appealing the town's denial of their *second* 8-30g application. This time they'd chosen what they thought was an ideal location: a half-acre lot across from the train station. But Conze's commission still objected to the project's density. In February 2012, after mediation talks between the two parties broke down, a superior court judge ruled in favor of the Stefanonis' proposal for a three-story apartment house. The judge concluded that the town had "provided no evidence of the harm that will occur or why this harm outweighs the need for affordable housing."[61] Unwilling to give up the fight, the town had filed for appeal, despite the mounting legal bills.[62]

The Stefanonis still had two other projects in litigation; both were more controversial because of their location in residential areas. But the couple was also fighting on a different front—and this made them all the more unpopular. The Stefanonis were determined to invalidate the town's much-celebrated 8-30g moratorium.

The moratorium provision under 8-30g is intended to reward towns that show progress in generating affordable housing. An incentive to produce housing, the moratorium gives qualifying towns a four-year breather to adjust to housing growth and plan for the future. Eligibility is determined through a complicated formula that assigns points for different types of affordable units. The state Department of Economic and Community Development (DECD) oversees the application process.

Evonne Klein's administration had looked into a moratorium during the uproar over Nearwater. After consulting with state officials, a study commission she worked with concluded that the points were not there.[63] "Nobody thought we had the moratorium—nobody," Klein says.

That changed once she left office in 2009. Without Klein, a Democrat, on the ballot, Republicans focused on regaining a majority on the board of selectmen. Their candidate for first selectman, David Campbell, the wealthy CEO of a chain of building-supply stores, easily won the post. And once in office, Campbell decided that the town ought to apply for the moratorium after all. Not just quietly, but covertly. He notified his fellow selectmen of the application but asked them to keep it secret so the Stefanonis wouldn't rush to submit more 8-30g applications in the meantime. "It is imparative [sic] we keep this to ourselves," Campbell wrote in an e-mail. "When we get the moratorium, we can have a party in public, but for now it is private."[64]

The Darien board of selectmen did have something new working in its favor. The Avalon apartment building appeared to be worth more moratorium points than previously thought. That was the opinion of Timothy Hollister, a Hartford lawyer who helped draft 8-30g and, because he frequently represents developers, has become an expert on the law. Campbell had Hollister's reasoning in writing, which was a potential leg up with the state.

But Campbell was soon reminded that, unlike in the corporate world, the public's business is not supposed to be conducted in private. The DECD declined to consider Darien's moratorium application until the town had properly published notice of its intent to apply, and made the application available to the public. If Darien wanted a shot at a moratorium, it would have to open up the paperwork to public scrutiny.

The Stefanonis were first in line to take a look. After scouring the application and comparing the town's claims to the official record, Peggy came up with enough questionable statements to fill a binder. This she did and sent it off to the state. The most significant discrepancy, and one that Hollister soon picked up on as well, involved Clock Hill Homes, the town-run condo development.

Moratorium rules require that any housing counted toward points must be restricted to households with incomes below 80 percent of the area median income. All thirty of the Clock Hill condos were initially sold to purchasers with incomes below the 80 percent mark. But the deed restrictions applying to *resales* did not explicitly limit incomes to the 80 percent threshold. In fact, the language suggested that incomes could float up as high as 115 percent of area median income.[65] For this reason, the Stefanonis argued, Clock Hill appeared ineligible for moratorium points. And without those points, Darien did not qualify for a moratorium.

Hollister echoed the Stefanonis' observations about Clock Hill's ineligibility in a letter to DECD's commissioner, Joan McDonald. But a month later, in October 2010, McDonald gave Darien the nod anyway. The town had its moratorium, which Campbell said would give them time to "get housing in the right places."[66]

The state had come up with its own interpretation of the deed restriction, one that was not the most obvious interpretation but became so, in the words of DECD housing specialist Michael Santoro, when you "put in one comma." Asked where that comma ought to go, Santoro then told me, "Actually, I think we took one out."[67] Comma or no comma, what next became clear was that the state's rather tortured interpretation of the deed restriction did not match that of Clock Hill Homes' own management. The Darien Housing Authority managed the property for the town. In response to media requests about the authority's understanding of the income limits, the executive director produced a 1997 letter from the former town counsel interpreting the income restrictions in the same way the Stefanonis and Hollister did.[68] These were, in fact, the guidelines that the housing authority followed. But, according to an e-mail communication between housing authority board members, the Campbell administration hadn't directly consulted with the authority about what it was putting in the moratorium application.[69]

Again, Hollister, as well as the Stefanonis, complained to the DECD. This time, the commissioner responded with a letter to Campbell demanding clarification. In reply, Darien's town counsel, John Wayne Fox, suggested that the housing authority simply needed to keep better records.[70] He provided the commissioner with a spreadsheet his office had prepared purporting to show that, regardless of how one interpreted the deed restrictions, the *actual* incomes of all Clock Hill owners were below the 80 percent threshold. "We found no evidence to support the unsubstantiated allegation that Darien Housing Authority permitted any sales to households whose income exceeds eighty percent of area median income," Fox wrote in a letter accompanying the spreadsheet.[71]

The spreadsheet only seemed to compound the confusion. Some of the incomes listed were so low that they looked like mistakes. Those numbers stood out like red flags to Hollister, who had represented affordable-housing developers on dozens of projects. "Gentlemen," he wrote in yet another e-mail to DECD and Darien officials, "from a first glance, we have a serious problem here."[72] Household incomes listed as low as $2,250 defied credulity, and suggested that "whoever did the income verification had no idea what he or she was doing. Public assistance alone would be far more than those numbers." He questioned the town's diligence in figuring in all income sources.

Internal e-mails obtained from the housing authority revealed that town officials had little on hand to work with. In one e-mail, the authority's executive director said that, for condo sales prior to when she came on the job in 2006, "the rat's nest of files" she'd inherited contained almost nothing in the way of documentation of buyers' incomes.[73]

But however the town counsel gathered and calculated the incomes, the spreadsheet satisfied Commissioner McDonald. In December 2010, she announced that the moratorium would stand. Hollister, in a final, tersely worded letter to the commissioner, objected to her acceptance of the figures, saying the department "should never accept data that, on its face, is plainly inaccurate."[74]

A testy McDonald retorted in an interview that whether the income numbers and other data were questionable was simply not DECD's concern. "We are not in the business of making determinations as to whether incomes are appropriate or not," she said. All that the statute required, she said, was that Darien certify that the incomes are correct. And Darien had done that.

The state seemed to have gone out of its way to see Darien safely to the finish line. Klein, for one, was baffled by what had transpired. When she was in office, "we were in hot pursuit of a moratorium because the community was up in arms," she says. "People were afraid of Stefanoni, and they were calling him a predatory developer. They wanted results right away. It was no secret that my administration was working on this problem. So if somebody thought we had the points for a moratorium, why didn't they say so?"

As it happened, a few months before granting Darien's moratorium, McDonald, an appointee of the outgoing Republican governor, M. Jodi Rell, had granted a similarly controversial housing exemption to another affluent Republican stronghold, the town of Greenwich. In that instance, at the request of the town's first selectman, McDonald permanently let Greenwich off the hook for twenty-four housing units it had promised to create two decades before as "payment" for thirteen acres of waterfront land turned over to the town by the state.[75] This decision came in spite of a visit from Greenwich's own housing authority chairman during which he implored the commissioner to instead force the town to live up to its obligation.[76] As it happened, Greenwich and Darien also shared the same town counsel, John Wayne Fox, a former legislator.

Did Hollister suspect a political favor in Darien's case? "I don't have any evidence," Hollister said, "but I see a result from a state agency that can't be explained by the data, and the mind wanders."

Fox laughed off the notion of political influence. As far as he was concerned, the spreadsheet numbers as presented were accurate. "There were some individuals who had limited incomes, and that's the extent of it," he said.[77]

Hollister let the matter drop. The Stefanonis did not. Their own 8-30g applications were unaffected by the moratorium, having been filed before it was approved. But they were convinced that Darien had obtained a reprieve it did not deserve. The couple filed yet another lawsuit—this time challenging both the town and the state—and pursued the moratorium question into superior court.

What the Stefanonis wanted was a declaratory judgment from the court overturning the moratorium. Lawyers for the state and the town wanted the case dismissed out of hand. They argued that the Stefanonis lacked "standing" to bring such a suit because they weren't aggrieved—that is, they hadn't suffered any direct harm as a result of the moratorium. In June 2012, the judge agreed, and dismissed the case. He offered no comment on the actual merits of the moratorium decision.[78]

This time, it was the Stefanonis who vowed to appeal.

EVEN AS THE MORATORIUM controversy continued to play out, bold allegations of discrimination emerged. Conze and the town planning and zoning commission were the target of a federal civil rights action filed by a former resident who, like the Stefanonis, had tried to turn his house lot into affordable housing. Unlike the Stefanonis, after his application was denied, this resident, Christopher Hamer, didn't have the wherewithal to fight for long. He was sued by neighbors who accused him of "blackmail," had to pay a lawyer, and wound up bankrupt. Hamer was now accusing the commission of denying projects like his in order to keep out black residents.

Conze's previous "virus" comment was cited in the complaint as proof of bias, as was his warning in a State of the Town address that the "demographic and economic forces generated by our immediate neighbors to our east and west cannot be taken lightly."[79] Hamer's attorney, John Williams, argued that, given that Darien's neighbors are the diverse cities of Norwalk and Stamford, Conze was clearly referring to African Americans. "He did everything but use the 'N' word," Williams told a local reporter.[80] Conze has declined to comment, but town counsel Fox has denied the allegations on his behalf.

Still, for all the controversy swirling around the actions of town officials, the Darien brand was showing signs of change. The public-housing expansion had broken ground. The US Department of Justice finally appeared satisfied: in the summer of 2012, after keeping an eye on the town for two years, federal officials announced they were closing their investigation.[81] And the Darien Housing Authority had very quietly adopted an official policy for verifying incomes and maintaining the waiting list for Clock Hill Homes.

"One small step for us," wrote the housing authority chair, Jennifer Schwartz, in an e-mail to her board. "One giant step for the town of Darien."

SIX

No Town Is an Island:
Ossipee, New Hampshire

I F LOCAL CONTROL IS a New England–wide mantra, in New
Hampshire, it is akin to a religion. Here, the many who worship
at its altar view it as deliverance from a singular evil: big government. This is the LIVE FREE OR DIE state, or what you might
call the New England version of the Wild West. Cross the New
Hampshire border and you can throw off your motorcycle helmet,
unbuckle your seat belt, and stock up on sales-tax-free liquor in
the state-run stores conveniently placed along the highway.* If you
happen to swing by the State House, bring your gun along—lawmakers recently declared that citizens have a right to bring their
concealed, loaded weapons right on into the spectators' gallery.

In New Hampshire, broad-based taxes are verboten.[1] School districts are small and plentiful. And towns enjoy hyper-representation
in the state legislature, which, with 424 elected lawmakers, is the
largest in the country. The prevailing culture of freedom and self-
sufficiency has bolstered New Hampshire's reputation as a low-tax,

---

* New Hampshire is the only state in the nation that does not require adults
to wear seat belts. Anyone under age eighteen is required to buckle up.

business-friendly, common-sense, live-and-let-live kind of place. State boosters package it as "the New Hampshire Advantage." The reality on the ground is a little more complicated, of course. For example, among the tradeoffs for foregoing both sales and income taxes are a heavy dependence on local property taxes and minimal government support for higher education (actually, the least in the nation).[2] The corollary to being known as a tax haven for affluent retirees is an aging-in-place phenomenon that is contributing to the state's rapidly aging population.[3] And if localized tunnel vision on the one hand helps preserve the down-home traditions that continue to define the state, it also breeds a "not our problem" mentality that is deeply resistant to regional cooperation on regional problems—including the need for cheaper housing.[4]

Another inconvenient truth is that New Hampshire, like the majority of the country, is not a "home rule" state. Although its state constitution does acknowledge a right of revolution, it does not actually authorize towns to govern themselves. Technically, towns must bow to the higher authority of the state legislature.[5] This means that, contrary to very popular opinion, towns really only have as much power as state law says they do. Yet the full-blown local-control orthodoxy tends to keep a fair amount of decision-making power at the local level. And even then, towns have been known to overreach. A prime example of this blind belief in local autonomy occurred in the Lakes Region town of Ossipee, when residents marched headlong into a battle that had already been fought and lost a decade before.

Nestled between the White Mountains and the Maine border, in the eastern middle of the state, Ossipee is a sprawling, sparsely developed, and fiercely independent town wrapped around three villages. Local is so local here that each of the villages—Center Ossipee, West Ossipee, and Ossipee Corner (home of the Carroll County courthouse, jail, and nursing home)—maintains its own fire district with its own tax rate. A drive around town offers a glimpse of the indigenous resistance to change: miles and miles of roadway remains unpaved. "When new people come to town, I welcome them, but with a caveat," says Harry Merrow, the chairman of the board of selectmen and a state representative. "I tell them, if you want lights and sidewalks and other things you had where you came from, you might as well go home now."

Even zoning was considered unnecessary until the 1980s. Then, in the thick of a population boom, the people of Ossipee decided it was time to put up some gates. Bejeweled with lakes and ponds, and rimmed by the magnificent Ossipee Mountain range, their town had attracted summer people since the late 1800s. Private cottages, sleepaway camps, and family campgrounds had gradually claimed the shores of Ossipee Lake and the Bearcamp River. But Ossipee hadn't seen anything like the flood of retirees, Massachusetts refugees, and second-home owners that came rushing in between 1970 and 1990. The town's population doubled during that period, to 3,300.[6] (The population has since crept up to 4,300.)

The region's premiere vacation area lay just to the west: Lake Winnipesaukee boasts roughly seventy square miles of water surrounded by marinas, resorts, and trophy homes. Ossipee Lake, no puddle itself at more than three-thousand acres, offered a less expensive alternative in a low-key town where social outings tended toward church suppers, weekend sap boils, and snowmobiling.* With development taking up just 7 percent of Ossipee's seventy-one square miles, newcomers to town could still imagine they'd stumbled onto undiscovered territory.[7] They could convince themselves that life in Ossipee would be simpler, that whatever complications they'd left behind would not follow them here.

---

* Ossipee Lake is not entirely within Ossipee's boundaries. It lies partially within the town of Freedom.

It was 2001 when an affordable-housing developer appeared on their doorstep. Bill Caselden was a partner in Great Bridge Properties, a three-year-old venture based in the southern-tier city of Manchester. Great Bridge was unusual in that it was one of the few for-profit entities that focused solely on affordable housing. Most developers won't bother with purely affordable projects because of the complex government compliance requirements and the stiff competition for the tax-credit financing that makes such projects financially viable.[8] But Caselden, a certified public accountant, had mastered the intricacies of tax-credit financing and deal structuring while working for the Reznick Group, a national accounting firm. His partner, Chris Davies, was a sticks-and-bricks expert. For a couple of guys wanting to start a business without a lot of money, partnering in a niche that relies more on competence than capitol seemed a logical move.

The pair hadn't come upon Ossipee haphazardly. When scouting potential development sites, they followed a stiff set of criteria, most of which were intended to minimize the usual objections to high-density development. They also needed a property seller willing to keep their purchase option open long enough for them to get through the lengthy approvals and financing process. And, of course, their projects only made sense in areas with a demonstrable need for below-market-rate housing. Given all of these conditions, when property offerings came their way, nine times out of ten, Caselden and Davies passed. But in Ossipee, they came across that rare exception. An open field of roughly nine acres in the village district of Center Ossipee, the site looked just about perfect.

Most significantly, the village district was one of the few areas in town served by municipal water and sewer, a big plus for a dense project. Also, the property sat at the intersection of two main roads (routes 25 and 16B) and directly off an exit of Route 16, a major artery that runs from the seacoast to the Lakes Region and on up through the White Mountains. Being nearly on top of the main commuter routes, the development would generate minimal traffic in the nearby village center, which consisted of a half-mile stretch of Main Street lined with white-clapboard municipal buildings, a former train station reborn as a cozy restaurant, and a few storefronts.

The property had other advantages: It was not in an historic district. It was not close to wetlands, the presence of which adds an extra round of regulatory hoops. And it did not abut a high-end neighborhood, thereby sparing Great Bridge the wrath of deep-pocketed homeowners and their lawyers.

As for market demand, Caselden had no doubts. When he surveyed Ossipee and the surrounding environs of Carroll County, he saw an area starved for decent, affordable rentals. The pressures of population growth had caused home prices and rents in the area to soar in the 1990s. Between 1999 and 2001 alone, the rent and utilities for a two-bedroom apartment in Carroll County increased by 17 percent, continuing a long, upward trend that would likely continue, given that vacancies were stuck well below the "normal" level of 5 percent. [9] Local wages had not kept up with the rent increases, as job growth in the tourism-driven economy had largely been confined to the low-wage realms of retail and restaurants.[10] Much of that job growth was in the resort town of Conway, about twenty miles north of Ossipee.

Ossipee did have a healthy quotient of well-to-do summer residents, but the town as a whole was hardly living large. The median household income was about $45,000; some 18 percent of families lived below the poverty level.[11] It was not uncommon for those among the working poor who couldn't make rent year-round to spend the warmer months living in tents.[12] Also pointing to an affordability problem was the state's waiting list for Section 8 vouchers, the federal program that provides rent subsidies for very low-income households. The list for Carroll County ran to more than two hundred names, more than a quarter of which were people from Ossipee.[13]

This was not to say that Ossipee needed a high-rise. The Great Bridge partners were thinking more along the lines of twenty-four apartments. They envisioned six colonial-style buildings, with a mix of one-, two- and three-bedroom apartments. This was a more expensive layout than, say, two buildings of twelve, because it required more walkways and building mechanicals. But Ossipee's zoning regulations set a maximum of four units in multifamily dwellings, and Caselden and Davies preferred to play by the rules. As a sweetener, they would cluster the buildings fairly close so that they could leave almost six acres untouched as open space.

The only potential obstacle to what otherwise looked like a winning plan was some puzzling wording in Ossipee's zoning ordinance. Multifamily housing was plainly identified as a permitted use in the village district—that wasn't the issue. The problem was that the ordinance seemed to require multifamily units to be in an *existing* building. Caselden read through the ordinance repeatedly to see if he'd missed something, but it still made no sense. Did the town really mean that new construction of multifamily housing was not allowed? He put the question to Ossipee's building inspector.

"His response was, 'No, that's not what they mean. That's crazy. Go to the zoning board and they'll give you a variance,'" Caselden recalls. "I mean, you read it and you thought it was a mistake."

IT WAS NO MISTAKE when the town of Chester, about sixty miles to the south, excluded multifamily housing from all five of its zoning districts. A bedroom community of Manchester, Chester (current pop. 5,000) had vigilantly preserved its colonial past. The town center was frozen in time, its cemetery the resting place for veterans of the Revolutionary War. Commerce and industry had passed Chester by, and townspeople had focused on perfecting a rural image—even if, by the 1980s, fewer than 5 percent of them actually made a living from the land.[14]

This primarily meant maintaining low density. Prior to the 1980s, in fact, multifamily housing was deemed so out of character for Chester that it wasn't allowed. Single-family homes were to occupy at least two acres; a duplex required three. Over time, this left few housing choices in Chester for people in lower-income brackets.

This was perhaps why George Edwards, a woodcutter at a local factory, found himself living in his parents' backyard in the early 1980s. Edwards, then in his thirties, had grown up in Chester and wanted to stay. But on his annual salary of $14,000, he couldn't afford to live anywhere but in a trailer without running water. He shared the one-bedroom trailer with his wife and three children. When someone in the family needed to use a bathroom, they had to cross the yard to Edwards's parents' house.[15]

In 1985, Edwards joined with some other low-income families and a local builder in a lawsuit aimed at forcing Chester to lift its ban on apartments. The builder, Raymond Remillard, had been trying unsuccessfully for years to obtain approvals for a forty-eight-unit apartment project on a twenty-three-acre property he owned along a major roadway. His plan included at least ten apartments for low- to moderate-income tenants. The lawsuit argued that by keeping out apartments, Chester was unfairly keeping out people in lower wage brackets.

Within a year of being sued, Chester reconsidered its position and revised its ordinance in a way that appeared more friendly to multifamily housing. But upon close examination, the revision proved little more than window dressing: the areas where multifamily housing was allowed and feasible still amounted to less than 2 percent of the land in town.[16] Remillard and the others continued to press their case. After the superior court ruled that Chester's ordinance was invalid, the town appealed. The state supreme court took up the matter.

At the heart of the standoff were these questions: Were towns obligated to consider regional needs when using their state-given zoning authority to control growth? Could Chester legally zone out the poor and leave the responsibility for housing people of lower incomes to other towns? In formulating its opinion, the state supreme court looked to wording in the state law that grants towns the power to set zoning regulations. Using language common to many states, the New Hampshire law sets fairly specific parameters around zoning authority.[17] Zoning regulations, it says, must serve "the purpose of promoting the health, safety, or the general welfare *of the community*" (emphasis added).[18] Chester read that charge through localized lenses that looked only as far as town borders. The town's zoning regulations were written to "maintain the rural nature of our town," selectman John Nucci would later say.[19]

Elliott Berry, lead counsel for the plaintiffs and a seasoned lawyer with New Hampshire Legal Assistance, took a longer view. His position, then and now, is that wholesale prohibitions on multifamily housing only promote the welfare of a select population—those able to afford a house on a few acres—and are deleterious to those of lower income levels. "Every time a town in a suburban area pulls up the drawbridge, it creates a greater temptation for other towns to follow," Berry says. "Each suburban community closes another door."

In 1991, the state supreme court came down on the side of the all-inclusive community. In a decision known as *Britton v. Chester*, which drew national attention, the court struck down Chester's multifamily housing ordinance as "blatantly exclusionary."* The court found that Chester's ordinance flew in the face of the state's

---

* Wayne Britton was another low-income plaintiff in the case.

"general welfare" provision by wrongfully excluding people of low to moderate incomes.

More significantly, the court clarified that the statute's reference to "community" should be interpreted to mean the broader community, of which a single town is only a part. Taking as its cue a seminal ruling in an exclusionary zoning challenge in New Jersey known as the *Mt. Laurel case*, the New Hampshire court found that all municipalities had an obligation to provide a realistic opportunity for people of lower incomes to obtain affordable housing:

> Municipalities are not isolated enclaves, far removed from the concerns of the area in which they are situated. As subdivisions of the State, they do not exist solely to serve their own residents, and their regulations should promote the general welfare, both within and without their boundaries.[20]

Housing advocates and many planners around the country hailed the Chester ruling as a blow to exclusionary zoning far and wide. A former president of the American Planning Association called it "the most important land-use decision in the last 10 years."[21] George Edwards, the woodcutter, said the outcome had made the long fight worthwhile.[22] A lawyer for the New Hampshire Municipal Association advised towns throughout the state to revisit their zoning ordinances to ensure that they provided more than "illusory opportunities" for apartment construction.[23] Fairness, it seemed, would now have to be part of the local zoning lexicon.

And then . . . almost nothing changed. New Hampshire towns continued to embrace ordinances that made it difficult, if not impossible, to build multifamily housing. Who was there to stop them? If *Britton v. Chester* provided the grounds for challenging exclusionary policies, developers proved uninterested in spending time and money in court. The Chester case had taken so long that, even though the decision ordered the town to allow Remillard to build his housing project, the real estate crash of the early 1990s prevented him from obtaining financing. The easier way for developers to win over towns was to play a different version of the same exclusionary game. They learned to target denser projects at people aged fifty-five and up—so-called 55-plus communities—which towns viewed as a boon because they didn't allow school-age children.

The landmark court decision barely even made an impact on the exclusionary culture in Chester itself. Between 1990 and 2000, the only new residential developments in town were single-family homes.[24] In a community survey conducted in 2005, 71 percent of respondents said they did not believe Chester, now among the highest-priced towns in the state, needed any affordable housing.[25] As of 2012, the town had a grand total of thirteen units of moderate-income housing, less than 1 percent of its housing stock.[26] Multifamily housing in general (not including duplexes) amounted to just 2 percent of all housing in town.

The scant supply of apartments is partly attributable to the absence of a municipal sewer, but a read through the Chester zoning regulations reveals other barriers. New multifamily housing is only permitted in what's called an "open space subdivision," which requires a minimum of twenty-five acres and a substantial set-aside of conservation land. Alternatively—and this should sound familiar—it may be created within an existing building.[27]

Ultimately, *Britton v. Chester* did prove to be "a useful decision," says Berry, but, he acknowledges, "not necessarily in producing housing in Chester."

THE SCENE IN OSSIPEE Town Hall was Caselden's worst nightmare: a zoning board of adjustment hearing attended by nearly a hundred people, all of whom were waiting for him. It was December 2002, and Caselden had come to ask the board for the variances Great

Bridge needed to get around the odd restriction of apartments to existing buildings. Seated among the audience members were at least two town selectmen, including Harry Merrow, the change-averse native. Although he was an Ossipee native with deep ancestral roots, Merrow had spent thirty years away, mostly living in Massachusetts, during his career as an electrical engineer. The profession took him all over the country and the world, and it ultimately allowed him to retire to his hometown while still in his fifties. Now, like nearly everyone else gathered here, he was unhappy about affordable housing invading his town. He thought it would bring in low-income outsiders with children, and in his view—one that ran contrary to *Britton* but was steeped in New Hampshire tradition—Ossipee was only responsible for seeing to the needs of its own people.[28]

Great Bridge's lawyer, Ken Viscarello, opened the discussion, by observing that Ossipee's brand of prohibition on multifamily housing was so unusual that, in sixteen years as a real estate lawyer in New Hampshire, he'd never seen one like it. He pointed out that the Great Bridge proposal was actually a less intensive use of the nine-acre property than zoning allowed. Under his interpretation of the regulations, they could have divided the land into almost thirty lots and put a house on every one.[29] Instead, they planned to preserve six acres as green space.

Someone asked if this project was subsidized housing. Caselden knew what was in people's heads—they heard the word "subsidized" or "affordable" and immediately envisioned the crime-ridden public housing projects built to warehouse the urban poor in the 1960s and '70s. He tried to explain that his proposal would in no way bear resemblance to the misguided projects of the past. For one thing, this was not government-run housing; Great Bridge would own the development and see to its upkeep. Rents would be lower than the market rate, but people would be required to show an ability to pay before they could live there. Residents would also have to pass a criminal-background check. And, as a for-profit entity, Great Bridge would not be exempt from paying property taxes.[30]

Caselden had barely finished his explanation when another Ossipee resident predicted that the development would be packed with as many as twenty-four kids, many of whom would likely be hanging around looking for trouble. Someone else said that, based on the total number of bedrooms, the number of kids would likely be closer to forty. A mother chimed in with a prediction that these kids, because they came from lower-income homes, were also going to require costly special-needs help in the town schools.[31]

A representative from the largest social-service agency in the area, Tri-County Community Action Program, spoke up to remind people that plenty of Ossipee residents would qualify for this housing. The audience was unaffected. Another resident, Jon Brown, said he had "moved up from Massachusetts to get away from this type of stuff." Jean Simpson, a homeowner who lived on an eight-acre property abutting the development site, echoed Brown's opinion: "I don't want this—it's why I moved here." Before she'd moved to the village, Simpson explained, she'd called town hall to ask about the zoning. "It seemed to be very strict, it seemed to be very well thought out," she said, "and it was a place that I wanted to be because we didn't allow for these types of things. I didn't think this was going to be an issue."[32]

The Great Bridge team was stunned. They were used to opposition, but people here weren't even trying to hide their prejudices. They didn't want multifamily housing. They assumed lower-income people from out of town were nothing but trouble and their kids laden with behavioral problems and learning disabilities.

Ossipee's unusual restriction on multifamily housing was clearly not a mistake.

When the public hearing resumed a week later, the zoning chairman, Mark McConkey, a local businessman, left no doubts on that point. By way of explaining his vote against the developer's application (which would finally be denied), McConkey pondered the ordinance's intent aloud. "It is my thought," he said, "that when this ordinance was written it was known at that time that this was exclusionary. It was written exactly for that reason."

He went on, "I believe the spirit of this ordinance was to deny the opportunity for multifamily housing to go forward in this town. I believe that's the intent of the ordinance whether it is right or wrong."[33]

McConkey's startling admission was as good as a gift, from Viscarello's perspective. First thing the next morning, he dispatched a paralegal to Ossipee. He wanted a copy of the hearing tapes before anything could happen to them. Two months later, after failed attempts to get the board to reconsider its denial, Great Bridge sued the town in superior court.

THE COMMONLY HELD NOTION that a community is only responsible for "its own" dates to New England's earliest days, when newly formed colonies adopted versions of the poor laws they left behind in England.[34] Towns were responsible for providing relief to their own poor residents, which made sense at a time when people didn't move around much. In Ossipee—a fairly self-sufficient community by the 1800s, with residents deriving most of what they needed from family farms, local mills, and a few stores—the town elders doled out assistance in the form of food, fuel, payment of medical bills, and work apprenticeships for children who couldn't live at home.[35] A strange face seeking assistance might be asked to provide proof of "settlement": his or her birthplace or evidence of long-standing status as a landholder or taxpayer. Those without proper settlement were not Ossipee's concern.

As Ossipee's population grew, seeing to the needs of the poor became an expensive enough proposition that the town eventually bought a farm where the needy could live and work. Figuring out which poor people "belonged" to Ossipee became more tricky as improved roadways and rail transit enabled people to move around more easily. By 1870, Ossipee and the surrounding towns had decided that support for the poor was an obligation better left to the county, which led to the building of a county farm.[36]

New Hampshire still has a poor law, now called a municipal welfare law. Municipalities remain obligated to "relieve and maintain" residents with nowhere else to turn.[37] (Relief typically amounts to subsistence benefits such as paying a heating bill, covering a month's rent, or stocking cupboards.) The "settlement" concept lasted some two hundred years, generally requiring that a welfare applicant have lived in town for at least a year.[38] In the 1980s, the state amended the welfare law to prohibit communities from turning away welfare applicants solely because they are new to town.[39] County government no longer plays a role in providing assistance.

This municipal obligation to extend even temporary assistance to "outsiders" still rankles in many corners of the Granite State. Where the old Yankee stoicism endures, hardship is not to be talked about but simply tolerated. As a former Ossipee selectman once declared, "The really poor" don't "come looking for welfare. They've lived here all their life. They make it somehow."[40]

As strong as that cultural reluctance to acknowledge need, however, is the prevailing notion of a singular responsibility to "our own." Merrow, for one, talks about his opposition to the Great Bridge complex in terms of "us" and "them." At the time the project was proposed, he says, he was concerned that the housing would attract outsiders who would come and apply for town welfare. In addition, "people here felt that it was being promoted by other towns to put it here so they wouldn't have to have it in their towns, and that raised hackles. I think towns should provide housing if their own people need it."

This is a fairly porous concept, however, given how much people move around these days. Like Merrow, young adults commonly leave the town in which they were born to pursue employment elsewhere. Those who do stick around their hometowns are very likely to commute elsewhere for work. Or perhaps they will move out of town for a period and then move back years later. All of this movement creates head-spinning confusion when it comes to trying to label people as belonging to one town or another. Do you only belong to the town in which you live, or do you also belong to the town in which you make a living? What if you were born in the town in which you work, but you live in the next town over? Which community then should call you one of its "own"? And would you or your elderly mother fall into the category of "carpetbaggers" if you were to seek affordable housing back in your hometown after years of living elsewhere?

New England's fragmented local government is not inclined to acknowledge our regional lifestyles. Even in rural Ossipee, about half the workforce commutes out of town, and they are traveling ever-greater distances. The average commute time as of 2003 was almost twenty-six minutes, up from twenty-one minutes in 1990.[41] The trend in Ossipee mirrors what has happened throughout Carroll County. In 2000, about a quarter of all commuters worked outside the county; nearly 7 percent traveled out of state, with most of those headed for Massachusetts.[42]

If communities are increasingly interdependent for jobs and services, they continue to govern in terms of what they perceive as best for their "own." "Towns sort of feel like islands even if their people work elsewhere, their own employees live elsewhere," says Theresa Kennett, program director for the Mt. Washington Valley Housing Coalition. "They don't feel the need to know what's going on beyond their borders." And it is homeowners who drive this mindset, out of their twin desires to buoy property values and, especially in New Hampshire, hold down property taxes.

In a state where school costs typically represent 65–70 percent of the local property-tax bill, homeowners tend to be hypersensitive to residential development that might drive up school enrollment.[43] Over the past decade, the resistance to family-oriented development contributed to the proliferation of age-restricted, kid-free housing—the so-called 55-plus communities—which grew by some 3,500 units in New Hampshire.[44]

Yet, as with fears about welfare-seeking carpetbaggers, taxpayers tend to let their imaginations run wild when confronted with potential housing development. Conventional wisdom holds that each new dwelling unit generates two or more school-age children, says Russell Thibeault, an economic and real estate consultant based in the Lakes Region. His own analysis disproves that assumption, however, finding instead that this math grossly overestimates kid counts.[45]

Using data collected by the US Census Bureau and comparing it against individual case studies, Thibeault concluded that the typical single-family home in New Hampshire generates 0.54 students—not even close to the two-per-house rule of thumb. The average rises with the number of bedrooms, reaching 0.81 in houses with four or more bedrooms. The same pattern holds for rentals—the more bedrooms, the more kids—but *overall*, rentals actually generate fewer students than do single-family homes because most apartments have only one or two bedrooms.

New Hampshire's school enrollment exploded during the 1990s, growing at twice the rate of the overall population. Thibeault maintains that the upsurge in children was *not* primarily linked to housing development, however. In fact, one study estimated that the number of homes under construction in the 1990s amounted to only half of what was needed to keep up with new jobs.[46] Instead, swelling classroom populations had more to do with demographic changes.

The baby-boomer generation (then between the ages of thirty-five and forty-nine) added more people during the 1990s than any other age category in the state, Thibeault says. As the age group most

likely to have children, these boomers—much more so than housing development—caused the unusual swell in school enrollment.

Now, with baby boomers aging out of their child-raising years,
school enrollment throughout much of the state has dropped off
sharply, particularly in rural areas like Carroll County.[47] And some
communities are finding that trying to bring down school spending by keeping out kids is a game of diminishing returns. At some
point, districts reach a floor of fixed expenses: state and federal
mandates, salaries and benefits, utilities and maintenance.[48]

At this point, New Hampshire needs *more* young families, not
fewer, argues Peter Francese, a demographic-trends analyst who
lives in the Seacoast region and founded *American Demographics
Magazine*. For the past five years, Francese has stood before audi-
ences in towns throughout New Hampshire (as well as on Cape Cod
and in Connecticut) warning residents that they are collectively
zoning their beloved state into future economic decline. In 2008,
he made his case in a locally distributed book called *Communities
and Consequences*, and in a companion documentary, available on
DVD.[49] "New Hampshire's demographic imbalance—a population
that is aging more rapidly than normal, combined with exceedingly slow growth and the exodus of too many young people—is
depleting the future workforce," he writes in *Communities*. "If
balance is not restored, it will slowly but surely strangle the state's
prospects for economic growth."[50]

The latest round of US census data showed that New Hampshire
now has the fourth-highest median age in the country. This is
largely because of the state's unusually high concentration of baby
boomers, not because of an outsized cohort of senior citizens.[51] But
those baby boomers are aging. And this makes the state's historically weak appeal to young adults in their twenties particularly
troubling. This age group declined by a startling 23 percent in the
1990s, mostly due to a dip in the birth rate during the 1970s. New
Hampshire has since been unable to attract enough new young

adults to fill the gap; the twentysomething population grew some during the last decade, but migration rates showed a net loss of 10 percent among this footloose age group.[52]

Kenneth Johnson, a senior demographer at the University of New Hampshire, places most of the blame for the decline in young adults on shifting birth rates and a slowdown in newcomers moving into the state during the recession in the last half of the decade. Francese believes the trend has been exacerbated by a housing climate that, by its lack of diversity, is inhospitable to young adults, especially compared to other regions of the country.[53] Unless New Hampshire can entice more young workers, he says, the future needs of baby-boomer senior citizens could overwhelm the state with demands for Medicaid and health care.

The New Hampshire Center for Public Policy projects that by 2030 "nearly half a million Granite Staters will be over the age of 65—a so-called 'silver tsunami,' representing almost one-third of the population."[54] As it happens, the phenomenon will be most evident in Ossipee's home of Carroll County. By that year, the county is expected to have a higher proportion of residents over the age of sixty-five—nearly half its population—than any other county in the state.[55]

For now, everything looks wonderful, says Francese. "We have a highly educated and highly skilled workforce—forty-five to sixty-four years is the biggest chunk of people in the population. So you say, 'It's not raining, why should we fix the hole in the roof?'

"But you look at the hole, and it's the deficit of people ages twenty-five to thirty-four. That hole is going to get larger if housing becomes less affordable."

WHEN *GREAT BRIDGE V. OSSIPEE* came before the state superior court, the judge didn't have to look much further than *Britton v. Chester* to conclude that Ossipee had overstepped its zoning authority. In a February 2005 ruling that cited Mark McConkey's bold statements about the town's exclusionary intent, the court ruled that Ossipee's zoning ordinance did not promote the general welfare of the community.[56] And in this case, community was defined as the breadth of Carroll County, a conclusion reached by the court through an analysis of commuter patterns.

"By making it economically infeasible for low-income households to live in the town, and by enacting zoning ordinances that preclude the development of affordable housing, the town has created a moat to keep out low-income households from both the county and other regions," the court concluded. "Such a scheme is clearly illegal."[57]

This was the first (and only) time Great Bridge had taken a town to court; Caselden preferred to avoid costly litigation. But in this instance, the owner of the development site was willing to wait it out with them, and Viscarello had persuaded them that they had a winning case. Costs associated with the court challenge meant Great Bridge had to spend another $4,700 per unit, a budgetary strain, but one they could bear. "It was senseless to add that much money to this project," Viscarello says, "but we felt that's what we had to do."

The resulting complex, called Ossipee Village, opened in July 2006. Since then, virtually none of the project opponents' worst imaginings have come true. At last check in 2011, fourteen school-age children—not forty—lived in the twenty-four-unit development. And not all residents were new to Ossipee—some had previously lived elsewhere in town.[58] Selectman Merrow confirms that the development has not resulted in a spike in welfare applications. Nor is it a magnet for crime.

"There have been no problems there," says David Senecal, the town zoning-enforcement officer. "It's nicely landscaped and well taken care of."

Tenants are a mix of newcomers and existing residents. Ossipee Village was a step up for Richard Woodworth, forty, who lived down the road at another apartment house before moving about five years ago. Then working at a health-care job that paid $9.25 an hour, Woodworth could afford his previous apartment, but, he said, "the upkeep there was, to be nice, horrendous. The management did have a guy come in and fix my windows one day while I was gone. My neighbor saw him sitting down watching TV in my apartment." Before checking out Ossipee Village, Woodworth had looked all over the area, from Wolfeboro to Conway, for another place that was both decent and affordable. "I was only finding what I consider substandard housing," he says, "and at the time my standards were pretty bloody low."

Jerry Carr, another tenant, was desperate for a place he could afford when he found out about Ossipee Village while searching the Internet. Then in his early seventies, Carr had been living in Gilmanton in a house owned by a relative, after what he describes as a long downward spiral in which his wife died of a sudden illness, the Massachusetts trucking company he worked for shut down, and he lost his house. In 2008, when the relative also ran into financial trouble, Carr was given just a few weeks to find another place to live. His pension and Social Security added up to an annual income of roughly $23,000, which did not give him a lot of options. "I had no idea where I was going to go," Carr says. "This place saved my life."

Since Ossipee Village opened, the recession has taken a toll on the town, shuttering some small businesses and claiming homes. Two houses adjacent to the complex were lost to foreclosure. Up the road in a small house on the corner of Main Street, Kim Altomare and her husband, Frank, have struggled with health problems and job losses. "Basically, we're the working poor," Altomare says. She and Frank were vocal opponents of the Great Bridge project—and hardship has not made her any more accepting of it.

Altomare acknowledges that the development has not disrupted the town. (She would have heard about any trouble on her police scanner.) And she recognizes many of the faces there. "Most of them are people around here who needed housing," she says. And yet, if she had it to do over again, she says, she would still oppose the project, simply because she wanted the land to remain undeveloped. "I understand we need workforce housing," Altomare says, "but not in my backyard, basically."

Britton v. Chester has proved no match on its own for such intransigence. In Elliott Berry's view, only the force of law can overcome people's kneejerk reactions to affordable housing as a threat to their environment. "You can educate until the cows come home," Berry says, "but you're only going to solve this problem with lawsuits and statutes." That is why, in 2008, after New Hampshire's workforce housing shortage had grown severe enough to worry the state's business lobby, and after years of study and debate, lawmakers finally wrote *Britton v. Chester* into law.[59] Their workforce-housing law echoes *Britton* with a requirement that all municipalities provide "reasonable and realistic opportunities" for workforce housing and that they allow it within a majority of the land area zoned for residential use.

Significantly, towns are only asked to ensure that their zoning regulations provide "opportunity"; they are not mandated to work toward a proscribed number of housing units. New Hampshire political realities demanded that the law adhere to the hallowed tradition of local control. "It is not our intent to create workforce housing everywhere," says George Reagan, program administrator at the New Hampshire Housing Finance Authority. "This approach creates an opportunity, then leaves it up to the market. If there's not growth and price pressure, then it wouldn't necessarily be built."

Individual communities may comply in any way they wish, which may mean not complying at all. Under the new law, however, recalcitrant towns run a higher risk of being challenged in court. The law sets up an expedited process for appeals of thwarted housing projects; a hearing must be held within six months. It's too soon to say whether this approach will stimulate more housing development—or whether it will even survive. Many lawmakers still view it as an intrusive mandate; *Britton* be damned, they have twice tried to amend the housing law to add an opt-out provision and, in direct defiance of the decision, officially define community as "the area within the boundaries of any municipality."[60] Pressure from the business community has kept the law intact so far. As of mid-2011, 45 towns out of 234 had adopted some sort of workforce-housing ordinance.

Even all these years after *Britton*, Berry remains optimistic. With demographic threats looming, he sees more people beginning to take the responsibilities articulated in both the Chester and Ossipee decisions seriously. "It's frustratingly slow, but it's happening," Berry says. "What's sad to me," he adds, "is I think New Hampshire municipalities originally had that economic diversity. The suburbanization of much of New Hampshire destroyed that, and it's going to take a long time to get that back."

CONCLUSION

J UST AS I WAS finishing up this book, the Connecticut Fair
Housing Center filed a federal lawsuit charging the Housing
Authority of Winchester with discrimination.[1] Located in a town
of roughly eleven thousand in the Litchfield hills, the Winchester
Housing Authority wields considerable clout in the state's northwestern region because it runs the Section 8 housing voucher
program for seventeen towns, including its own community.*
This so-called "Rental Assistance Alliance" consists wholly of
predominantly white towns—Roxbury among them—which together form a misshapen doughnut around the racially diverse
city of Torrington.

The lawsuit accuses the housing authority of refusing to provide Section 8 applications to people who don't live in one of the
seventeen towns, a residency requirement that violates federal
regulations. The plaintiff is an African American mother of six
who was in desperate need of stable housing when she inquired
about getting on the Winchester housing authority's waiting list.
The woman, who then lived in the city of Hartford, claims that the

---

* Section 8 is a federally funded housing-assistance program for the very
low income, the elderly, and the disabled. It is administered through local housing authorities, which distribute vouchers to qualified applicants.
The vouchers are good for rental subsidies (paid directly to landlords) and
may be used in the private market, not just in subsidized housing projects.

Winchester authority's staff person refused to send her a Section 8 application. Further, she claims, the staffer discouraged her from moving to Winchester by saying there were no jobs and steered her instead toward housing programs in Torrington and other cities.

The authority says the residents-only rule was a temporary measure intended to cut costs. But the Fair Housing Center believes the change was a response to a significant increase in the number of African American applicants on Winchester's Section 8 waiting list. The lawsuit accuses the authority of deliberately upending the "mobility and free-choice housing goals" of the Section 8 program by using residency requirements that ensure "that overwhelmingly-white communities remain overwhelmingly white." In all but one of the Rental Assistance Alliance communities, whites account for 94–100 percent of households.

The same week this lawsuit was filed, segregation also made the national news, with the focus this time on separation by class. A Pew Research Center report concluded that neighborhoods in the country's thirty largest metropolitan areas have become increasingly segregated by income.[2] Since 1980, the percent of wealthy households located in high-income neighborhoods has doubled—put another way, wealth is increasingly concentrated in fewer neighborhoods. Poor households are also more likely to be grouped together, while mixed-income neighborhoods are shrinking. Researchers cited rising income inequality as the primary factor behind the trend. But a *Washington Post* story noted that an earlier study out of Stanford University pointed to another and longer-term dynamic at play: widespread restrictions on minimum lot sizes, which prevent cheaper housing from being built.[3]

Both stories—the discrimination lawsuit and the study of rising income segregation—underscored how exclusion at the local level is drawing attention in a way that it has not since the 1970s. I believe the focus is spurred by two forces. One is the country's deepening economic divide—what Occupy Wall Street dubbed the

99 percent versus the 1 percent—which has triggered a national discussion about inequality. The second is the collapse of the housing market. The resulting foreclosure crisis devastated minority neighborhoods targeted by subprime lenders and highlighted how segregated we really are.

Prior to the recession, any talk about the evils of exclusionary zoning tended to omit references to social stratification. "Smart growth" proponents focused on the relationship between low-density zoning and suburban sprawl. Economists talked about the link between burdensome zoning restrictions and higher housing costs. Now that the cultural winds have shifted, at least one social-policy think tank is bluntly attacking restrictive zoning for keeping poor students out of good schools. And after decades of avoiding concerted action on residential integration, the federal government is playing hardball with wealthy, highly segregated Westchester County, New York, which was found to have accepted federal housing funds without complying with fair-housing mandates.[4]

If history is any guide, renewed attention alone is unlikely to put much of a dent in the fortress mentality. After all, towns have vehemently defended exclusionary practices as their right for decades—if not publicly, then covertly, and sometimes illegally. In addition to maintaining sharp limitations on multifamily housing, the most change-averse communities are known for enforcing residents-only policies and parking bans that keep outsiders away, flouting fair-housing laws, and using costly litigation to wear down affordable housing developers (a strategy known as "death by delay"). These practices have persisted in spite of court rulings reminding towns that their zoning must reflect regional needs. And they continue to butt up against affordable-housing laws that override unnecessarily restrictive zoning regulations. If these laws have generated housing that would otherwise not have been built, progress has still been slower than expected because of towns' ongoing willingness to fight even the most well-conceived projects, and their disinterest in planning for such housing on their own. As Paul McMorrow, a *Boston Globe* columnist, once observed, while the Massachusetts affordable-housing law, 40B, "is a great tool for cracking individual towns' anti-development zoning codes, the law is doing little to soften the hardened attitudes on the macro level that birthed the law in the first place."[5]

What may instead bring about some loosening of restrictions are the country's sweeping demographic changes. These, along with rising energy prices and concern about climate change, are driving a profound shift in market demand. The following indicators suggest that the US housing market is ripe for an about-face, back from the edges of the crabgrass frontier.

AGING BOOMERS AND YOUNG MILLENNIALS

The baby boom generation, that outsized cohort born between 1946 and 1964, has been the chief caretaker of the single-family subdivisions that for so long symbolized the American Dream. As the boomers now head into retirement, they are looking to unload the family home and move into smaller, more-manageable quarters. Convenience is their new watchword.

Meanwhile, another major slice of the population, the so-called millennials, born between 1980 and 2000, is heading out on its own. And this younger generation is far more drawn to dense, walkable communities than to auto-dependent suburban living. They aren't rejecting suburbs outright, but the kind of suburbs they're looking for aren't of the sprawling variety.[6] One reason is that millennials don't drive cars in the same numbers as previous generations—and they don't want to.

These preferences were borne out in a 2011 survey by the National Association of Realtors. The survey asked a broad spectrum of consumers whether they would prefer to live in a community consisting solely of single-family homes on large lots, and without sidewalks or public transportation, or, conversely, in a community with a variety of housing types, businesses, and nearby transportation. The majority (56 percent) preferred the more varied option, but millennials and boomers stood out as showing the strongest predilection for denser living.[7]

A MISMATCH IN THE HOUSING MARKET

America has more big houses than it needs—or wants. One recent study found that the oversupply totals around 40 million compared to consumer demand.[8] According to the National Association of Realtors, only 25 percent of Americans want a home on a large lot, yet that type of housing accounts for 43 percent of the supply.[9] The market is hungry for apartments, condominiums, and small homes, if zoning restrictions would only get out of the way. Converting all those unwanted McMansions into multifamily housing may be a start.

WALKABILITY IS WORTH MORE

Living preferences have shifted to such a degree that housing in walkable locations is becoming more valuable than housing set away from town centers. A Brookings Institution study of real estate values in the Washington, DC, metropolitan area confirmed that neighborhoods there increase in value according to how walkable they are.[10] This pattern has helped boost the popularity of transit-oriented development. More communities are showing interest in leveraging their transit stations to attract compact, mixed-use development that can bring vibrancy to often underutilized locations. Some states, including Massachusetts and Connecticut, have incentive programs in place to encourage towns to pursue high-density transit villages.

IF THESE DEMOGRAPHIC SHIFTS will likely refocus housing development around smaller, more densely sited options, they won't necessarily lock in affordability. In all likelihood, if transit neighborhoods take off and values rise, exclusion is likely to prove the rule all over again. The result will be that the lower-income households who are the most dependent on public transit will have to live farthest away. Decisions as to whether and how to accommodate a mix of incomes will continue to rest with local zoning authorities.

As the region's population becomes increasingly gray, local officials may take this obligation more seriously. This is already happening in some towns—typically the ones with professional, forward-thinking planning staffs. But if history is any guide, most towns will still have to be prodded out of their parochialism by laws and lawsuits. Willful blindness persists in the face of growing evidence of the damaging, long-term impacts of exclusion, despairs the demographer Peter Francese. "This is a world in which facts are irrelevant," he says. "I've explained over and over again that workforce housing is not Section 8 housing with welfare recipients packed in there. They won't believe it. And God forbid there be some black people in there!" Still, Joan Carty, the president of the Housing Development Fund, a community development institution in Stamford, Connecticut, finds reason for optimism in signs of incremental progress—and, given the countervailing forces, even incremental progress is still progress after all. "I used to think it was just a matter of political will, finding a nucleus of people who thought their towns would benefit from affordable housing, and then working through them to get it done," Carty says. "I don't think that anymore. . . . Our society has shifted to a more polarized, homogenized place. That is now the idea of what success looks like."

ACKNOWLEDGMENTS

T HIS BOOK WAS A years-long undertaking—which tells you something about the pace at which I write. It was as much of a marathon for my family as for me. They have kindly endured the ever-growing piles of books and binders, the late dinners and lengthy phone conversations, the lost days when it seemed I might never separate from my laptop. I am most grateful for their patience and encouragement, especially from my husband, Tim. It was Tim who helped me shape the initial idea for the book, hooked me up with my agent, and aided in polishing the proposal. Perhaps he wouldn't have done so much to get this book off the ground if he'd known how long it would take me to finish it! But if he had any regrets, he never once let on. This book is for him.

Many thanks to the National Association of Real Estate Editors, a professional organization of which I am a member, and to Professor George Harmon of Northwestern University's Medill School of Journalism for awarding me a 2008 Bivins Fellowship grant to help underwrite my research. I also received wise counsel from my colleagues at the American Society of Journalists and Authors.

I am indebted to Lynn Johnston, my agent, who embraced this idea from the start and worked tirelessly to make the book happen. Susanne Althoff, the editor of the *Boston Globe Magazine*, helped move the project along by publishing my article about resistance to cottage housing, which ultimately evolved into chapter 2. Special thanks to Amy Caldwell, my editor at Beacon Press, for her valuable insights and kind support when a serious health issue set me back.

My coursework in Fairfield University's master's program in American Studies provided considerable inspiration. Thanks in particular to Dr. Kurt Schlichting, who teaches a great course in urban/suburban sociology. As my master's thesis advisor, Dr. Schlichting allowed me to accomplish two objectives at once by approving my book subject as my thesis topic.

The staff at the Moakley Archive, at Suffolk University in Boston, helped me track down the materials I was after.

Daphne and Bob Bruemmer, Nannette Silva, Darren Prevost, and my dear parents, Ferd and Myrna Prevost, were kind enough to put me up when I was out on the road. Thanks to Peter Francese and David Fink for their encouragement. And thanks to the *New York Times* for giving me space to write about real estate.

NOTES

Unattributed direct quotes are from the author's own interviews.

INTRODUCTION

1. Lisa Prevost, "Resisting 'Affordable' Homes in Darien," *New York Times*, November 13, 2005.

2. The forty years Engler was referring to is the span of time since Massachusetts adopted Chapter 40B, the law that makes it harder for suburban communities to reject affordable housing. The history of this law is discussed in chapter 2.

3. Carol Morello, "Study: Rich, Poor Americans Increasingly Likely to Live in Separate Neighborhoods," *Washington Post*, August 1, 2012.

4. Myron Orfield, *American Metropolitics: The New Suburban Reality* (Washington, DC: Brookings Institution, 2002), 1.

5. Alan Zibel, "Despite Falling Prices, Housing Burden Still High for Middle Class," *Developments* blog, *Wall Street Journal*, February 24, 2012.

6. "America's Rental Housing: Meeting Challenges, Building on Opportunities," Joint Center for Housing Studies of Harvard University, April 2011, http://www.jchs.harvard.edu.

7. Robert Clifford, "The Housing Bust and Housing Affordability in New England: An Update of Housing Affordability Measures," New England Public Policy Center, Federal Reserve Bank of Boston, Discussion Paper 10–1, June 2010, http://www.bos.frb.org.

8. Barry Bluestone and Chase Billingham, "The Greater Boston Housing Report Card 2011: Housing's Role in the Ongoing Economic

Crisis," Dukakis Center for Urban and Regional Policy, Northeastern University, Boston, October 2011, http://www.northeastern.edu/dukakiscenter.

9. Lisa Prevost, "Affordable Housing Back in Play," *New York Times*, June 7, 2012.

CHAPTER ONE

1. Lisa Prevost, "What a Difference an Acre Makes," *New York Times*, August 26, 2007.

2. Mandy Ruggeri, "You Call This a Suburb? Where's Washington's Stoplight?" *Republican-American* (CT), August 8, 2004.

3. Lisa Prevost, "The Call of Converted Barns," *New York Times*, September 29, 2011.

4. Miller bought his first farmhouse in Roxbury in 1947 and wrote *Death of a Salesman* (published a year later) in a shack on the property. Elizabeth Maker and Bruce Weber, "Arthur Miller's Refuge Amid the Pines," *New York Times*, February 20, 2005; John Addyman, "Roxbury Honors Arthur Miller," VoicesNews.com, May 14, 2005.

5. Arthur Miller, *Timebends: A Life* (New York: Grove Press, 1987), 502.

6. Inge Morath and Arthur Miller, *In the Country* (New York: Viking Press, 1977).

7. Henrietta Rio R. MacKinnon Raikes vs. Town of Roxbury and Zoning Commission of the Town of Roxbury, Freedom of Information Commission, Report of Hearing Officer, Docket FIC79–107, September 12, 1979.

8. Joe Foster, "Town Split Open Over Shopping Center," *New Milford (CT) Times*, August 30, 1979.

9. I. M. Wiese and Henrietta Rio R. MacKinnon Raikes v. Roxbury Zoning Commission, Ct. Superior Court, Judicial District of Litchfield, Memorandum of Decision, January 19, 1981.

10. Foster, "Town Split Open Over Shopping Center."

11. *Raikes v. Roxbury.*

12. Irina Aleksander, "Graydon Carter's Better Half," *New York Observer*, June 15, 2010.

13. Allan Mallach, *A Decent Home: Planning, Building, and Preserving Affordable Housing* (Chicago: American Planning Association Planners Press, 2009), 160–62; J. John Palen, *The Suburbs* (New York: McGraw-Hill, 1995), 38–41.

14. Kenneth T. Jackson, *Crabgrass Frontier: The Suburbanization of the United States* (New York: Oxford University Press, 1985), 242.

15. Ibid., 196–97.

16. Ibid., 208.

17. Quoted in Michael N. Danielson, "The Politics of Exclusionary Zoning in Suburbia," *Political Science Quarterly* 91, no. 1 (Spring 1976): 11–12.

18. These rulings are discussed in greater detail in chapter 6.

19. Dennis Heffley and MaryJane Lenon, "Zoning: Can a Barrier to Entry Open a Road to Educational Gains?" *Connecticut Economy* (Summer 2004): 5.

20. Edward L. Glaeser and Bryce A. Ward, "The Causes and Consequences of Land Use Regulation: Evidence from Greater Boston," *Journal of Urban Economics* 65 (2009): 265–78.

21. *Large-Lot Housing Construction in the Greater Boston Metropolitan Area*, Center for Real Estate, Housing Affordability Initiative, Massachusetts Institute of Technology, January 2006, http://web.mit.edu/cre.

22. Edward Glaeser, *Triumph of the City: How Our Greatest Invention Makes Us Richer, Smarter, Greener, Healthier, and Happier* (New York: Penguin Press, 2011), 166.

23. Alice Tessier, "Roxbury Panel Backing 4-Acre Minimum Lot Size," *Litchfield County (CT) Times*, July 12, 2007.

24. Roxbury Plan of Conservation and Development, 2009 Amendments, Section 2—Conditions and Trends, http://www.roxburyct.com.

25. Megan Broderick, "Bigger Lots, Slower Growth: Roxbury Zoning Proposal Raises Concerns," *Republican-American*, July 23, 2007.

26. Barbara Loecher, "Rural Towns in State's Northwest Transformed in 1980's," *New York Times*, July 7, 1991.

27. Frederick Ungeheuer, with Lewis and Ethel Hurlbut, *Roxbury Remembered* (Oxford, CT: Connecticut Heritage Press, 1989), 42.

Roxbury's zoning regulations do make provision for affordable housing but only by special permit, and the conditions are quite onerous.

28. Prevost, "What a Difference an Acre Makes."

29. Ungeheuer, *Roxbury Remembered.*

30. John Addyman, "Affordable Housing Dominates Talk on Roxbury POCD," VoicesNews.com (CT), September 12, 2007.

31. "Roxbury and the Challenge of Change," editorial, *New York Times,* September 9, 2007.

32. Dan McGuinness, *Affordable Housing: An Introduction to Affordable Housing in the Northwest Corner of Connecticut,* Northwestern Connecticut Council of Governments, 2007, http://www.nwctplanning.org.

33. Frank Juliano, "Most Towns Have Fewer Students in Schools," *Connecticut Post,* July 9, 2011; Regine Labossiere, "Connecticut's White Population Tied For Third Place As Nation's Oldest," *Hartford Courant,* September 23, 2009.

34. Keith M. Phaneuf, "Report: Aging Workforce Threatens State's Economic Recovery," *Connecticut Mirror,* May 24, 2012.

35. Projections of Booth Free School Enrollment, Connecticut's Region 12 School District, fax to author, provided by Superintendent's Office, March 23, 2010.

36. Connecticut State Department of Education, Bureau of Grants Management, 2010–11 Net Current Expenditures per Pupil, http://www.sde.ct.gov/sde.

37. "Connecticut Still At Bottom In Attracting, Keeping 25–34 Year-Olds," policy brief, Partnership for Strong Communities, June 22, 2011, http://pschousing.org.

38. 2010 Affordability Study, Partnership for Strong Communities, http://pschousing.org/. The ranking of communities was based on the size of the gap between the state median income ($65,686) and the income required to qualify for a mortgage on the median-priced house in each community. In Roxbury, that gap amounted to more than $180,000. (The study's formula assumed a thirty-year mortgage with an interest rate of 4.5 percent and a ready down payment of 10 percent.)

39. McGuinness, *Affordable Housing.*

40. Several towns in the northwest corner do have active, volunteer-run groups dedicated to creating affordable housing. These groups have made considerable headway in the towns of Kent, Cornwall, and Sharon.

41. Tessier, "Roxbury Panel."

42. Minutes, Roxbury Zoning Commission, July 9, 2007, http://www .roxburyct.com.

43. Prevost, "What a Difference an Acre Makes."

44. Minutes, Roxbury Zoning Commission, April 14, 2008, http://www .roxburyct.com.

45. Memorandum to Jim Conway, chairman, Roxbury Zoning Commission from Peter Filous, chairman, Roxbury Planning Commission records, Roxbury, CT, July 29, 2011.

46. Roxbury already has a Conservation Subdivision regulation that allows for houses on slightly smaller lots (25 percent less than the minimum), provided that at least one-third of the subdivision's total acreage is set aside as open space. The purpose is not to increase density and/ or affordability, however, as the total number of houses cannot exceed that of a standard subdivision. The regulation has never been used.

CHAPTER TWO

1. Town of Easton Chapter 40B Affordable Housing Production Plan, May 2005, 23, http://www.easton.ma.us.

2. The average household size in Easton (2.62 in 2000) inched upward toward the end of the last decade. Economists say this was largely due to the recession: more young adults were living with their parents, and some people who lost homes to foreclosure moved in with friends or relatives.

3. "Quick Takes: Single People," Catalyst.org, April 2012.

4. The income restrictions for 40B aren't really targeted at minimum-wage workers. (This is a criticism of 40B—that it doesn't reach down low enough on the income scale.) The rules require ownership housing to be priced at a level affordable for buyers earning no more than 80 percent of area median income. According to the Boston-based

Citizens' Housing and Planning Association, as of 2011, that translated to a maximum of about $45,000 for a single-person household in the Greater Boston area and about $51,000 for two people.

5. From data compiled by William Raveis Real Estate. The median sale price as of the end of June 2012 was $406,000; www.raveis.com.

6. In order to cover the cost of selling a portion of a housing development at artificially low levels, developers typically either apply for funding from the limited pot of government-subsidy and financing programs and/or build the market-rate portion of the project at a higher density, thereby generating more revenue.

7. Voluntary Petition for Chapter 7 Bankruptcy, filed by Charles M. Mirrione, US Bankruptcy Court, District of Massachusetts, April 10, 2011, http://www.pacer.gov.

8. *Richardson, Olmsted, Others and the North Easton Historic Village District,* Easton Historical Society, 1990, 3, eastonhistoricalsociety.org.

9. Vicki-Ann Downing, "Easton School Plan Causes Uproar," *Enterprise* (Brockton, MA), October 9, 2008.

10. Bonnie Heudorfer and Barry Bluestone, "The Greater Boston Housing Report Card 2006–2007: An Assessment of Progress on Housing in the Greater Boston Area," Boston Foundation and Citizens' Housing and Planning Association, 8.

11. Annual Report, Town of Easton, 2007, 143–50, http://www.easton.ma.us.

12. Ibid., 76, 150.

13. Vicki-Ann Downing, "Denied in Easton, Developer to Try Housing Plan Elsewhere," *Enterprise*, May 24, 2007.

14. "Cozy, Sensible, Unwelcome," editorial, *Boston Globe*, December 14, 2007.

15. Gregory Norman, "Public Input Needed on Cottages Project," letter to the editor, *Enterprise*, October 2008.

16. John J. Palen, *The Suburbs* (New York: McGraw-Hill, 1995), 36–42.

17. Julie Campoli and Alex S. MacLean, *Visualizing Density* (Cambridge, MA: Lincoln Institute of Land Policy, 2007), 11.

18. Palen, *The Suburbs*, 33.

19. Peter O. Muller, *Contemporary Suburban America* (New York: Prentice-Hall, 1981), 33–35.

20. Dona Brown, *Inventing New England: Regional Tourism in the Nineteenth Century* (Washington, DC: Smithsonian Institution, 1995), 138–42.

21. Village of Euclid v. Ambler Realty Co., 272 US 365—Supreme Court 1926, http://caselaw.lp.findlaw.com.

22. Richard F. Babcock and Fred P. Bosselman, *Exclusionary Zoning: Land Use Regulation and Housing in the 1970s* (New York: Praeger, 1973), 8.

23. Robert M. Fogelson, *Bourgeois Nightmares: Suburbia, 1870–1930* (New Haven, CT: Yale University Press, 2005), 154; Alexander von Hoffman, "To Preserve and Protect: Land Use Regulations in Weston, Massachusetts," Joint Center for Housing Studies, Harvard University (November 2010): 11, www.jchs.harvard.edu.

24. Von Hoffman, "To Preserve and Protect," 11.

25. Christopher B. Leinberger, *The Option of Urbanism: Investing in a New American Dream* (Washington, DC: Island Press, 2008), 25–29.

26. Douglas S. Massey and Nancy A. Denton, *American Apartheid: Segregation and the Making of the Underclass* (Cambridge, MA: Harvard University Press, 1993), 56–57.

27. Alan Mallach, *A Decent Home: Planning, Building, and Preserving Affordable Housing* (Chicago: American Planning Association, 2009), 35–37.

28. Vina M. Aylmer to Sen. John Joseph Moakley, 1969, Moakley Archive, Suffolk University, Boston.

29. Typed copy of speech presented by Senator Moakley before the State Senate, August 1969, Moakley Archive, Suffolk University, Boston.

30. Transcript of editorial delivered by L. L. Thompson, area vice president, WBZ Radio-TV, and Jim Lightfoot, general manager, WBZ Radio, August 11, 1969, Moakley Archive, Suffolk University, Boston.

31. Rachel G. Bratt, "Overcoming Restrictive Zoning for Affordable Housing in Five States: Observations for Massachusetts," Citizens Housing and Planning Association, February 10, 2012.

32. Lynn Fisher, "Reviewing Chapter 40B: What Gets Proposed, What Gets Approved, What Gets Appealed, and What Gets Built?" Rappaport Institute Policy Brief, November 2008.

33. Some Chapter 40B regulation revisions came in response to a 2006 report by the state inspector general that found that some developers had understated their profits in order to take a higher margin than the 20 percent allowed under the law. Any profits in excess of 20 percent are supposed to be paid to the municipality.

34. Vicki-Ann Downing, "Easton Leads Anti-40B Foes," *Patriot Ledger* (Quincy, MA), June 30, 2010.

35. Paul McMorrow, "Smart Growth Funds Running Out," *Common-Wealth*, December 29, 2011. Connecticut has a similar program, known as HOMEConnecticut, which encourages towns to designate high-density "incentive housing zones."

36. Edward L. Glaeser, "Young Workers Can't Afford Homes in the State," *Boston Globe*, June 14, 2012.

37. William H. Frey, "The Uneven Aging and 'Younging' of America: State and Metropolitan Trends in the 2010 Census," Metropolitan Policy Program at Brookings, June 2011, 16–17, http://www.brookings.edu.

38. Barry Bluestone, "Sustaining the Mass Economy: Housing Costs, Population Dynamics, and Employment," Center for Urban and Regional Policy, Northeastern University, May 2006, http://iris.lib.neu.edu.

39. "Cottage Housing," Municipal Research and Services Center, http://www.mrsc.org.

40. Rus Lodi, "Zoning for Backyard Cottages Taking Hold in Seattle," Massachusetts Foundation for Growth blog, June 30, 2011, http://www.massgrowth.net.

41. Sara Lin, "The Newest Cottage Industry," *Wall Street Journal*, July 18, 2008. Chapin has written a book on the subject: *Pocket Neighborhoods: Creating Small-Scale Community in a Large-Scale World* (Newtown, CT: Taunton Press, 2011).

42. Conforti's short documentary, *Not In My Back Yard*, can be viewed on Vimeo: http://vimeo.com/15708304.

43. Vicki-Ann Downing, "Foreclosed Homes a Reality Check for Easton Developers," *Enterprise*, November 24, 2008.

44. Vicki-Ann Downing, "Easton Property Where Cottage Style Houses Planned Going to Foreclosure," *Enterprise*, June 25, 2009.

45. Under the terms of 40B, all 113 apartments will count toward the town's 10 percent affordable-housing goal because they are rentals.

46. Record of vote taken at Special Town Meeting, April 5, 2010, Office of the Easton Town Clerk. "Community Preservation Needs to Regain State Support," *Enterprise*, October 12, 2011. The Community Preservation Act authorizes communities to create a Community Preservation Fund through a surcharge of up to 3 percent of the real estate tax levy on real property. The funds must be used for open space protection, historic preservation, and/or the provision of affordable housing. Funds are matched by the state.

47. Justin Graeber, "Easton Leaders Hope Shovel Shop Development Leads to Downtown Revitalization," *Enterprise*, December 27, 2011.

48. Gina B. Dailey, director of Comprehensive Permit Programs, Mass-Housing, to Iqbal Ali, Saw Mill Pond Village LLC, Town of Easton website, March 1, 2012, www.easton.ma.us.

CHAPTER THREE

1. David A. Fahrenthold, "Filling a Faraway Niche: Even in Maine, Latinos' Future Affects Economy," *Washington Post*, April 8, 2006.

2. "Wild Blueberry Acres by Counties," statistics prepared by David E. Yarborough, Extension blueberry specialist, University of Maine Cooperative Extension, http://umaine.edu/blueberries.

3. Maine Center for Economic Policy, "The Growing Latin American Influence: Opportunities for Maine's Economy," 2009, http://www.mecep.org.

4. Craig Idlebrook, "Latinos Putting Down Roots Downeast," *Working Waterfront* (ME), September 1, 2008, http://www.workingwaterfront.com.

5. Community Profile of Milbridge, ME. Prepared under the auspices of the National Marine Fisheries Service, Northeast Fisheries Science Center. For further information, contact Lisa.L.Colburn@noaa.gov. Also, Mary Anne Clancy, "The New Face of Milbridge: Washington

County Town Addresses Challenges as Migrant Population Rises," *Bangor (ME) Daily News,* June 16, 2001.

6. Jeff Clark, "Invisible Mainers," *Down East,* August 2008, http://www.downeast.com.

7. Pam Belluck, "Mixed Welcome as Somalis Settle in a Maine City," *New York Times,* October 14, 2002.

8. Fahrenthold, "Filling a Faraway Niche."

9. Labor contractors are notorious for putting workers in substandard housing. The contractors recruit workers for their employer clients and often offer free housing as a recruiting incentive.

10. "Washington County Homeownership Facts 2009," MaineHousing, Maine State Housing Authority, http://www.mainehousing.org.

11. Henry O. Pollakowski, "Housing Affordability in Maine: Taking Stock," MIT Center for Real Estate, March 4, 2009, http://web.mit.edu/cre.

12. Washington Hancock Community Agency, 2008 Needs Assessment, http://www.whacap.org/resources.

13. Dick Fickett, owner/manager of Saybrook Apartments, author interview August 16, 2011. Milbridge also has some subsidized housing for the elderly; it too stays full.

14. John Wiltse, senior operations director, PathStone Corporation, author interview October 24, 2011.

15. One of the more recent and comprehensive studies was conducted by MIT's Center for Real Estate: Henry O. Pollakowski, David Ritchay, Zoe Weinrobe, "Effects of Mixed-Income, Multi-Family Rental Housing Developments on Single-Family Housing Values," April 2005, http://web.mit.edu/cre. The study analyzed the impact over time of seven large-scale, mixed-income, multifamily rental developments that were built in neighborhoods of single-family homes in the Boston metropolitan area. The conclusion in all seven cases was that the high-density developments *did not* affect the value of surrounding homes.

16. Sandra Dinsmore, "New Sardine History Museum Opens in Jonesport," *Working Waterfront,* September 1, 2008. Also: Katharine Q.

Seelye, "In Maine, Last Sardine Cannery in the U.S. Is Clattering Out," *New York Times*, April 3, 2010.

17. Ann W. Acheson, "Poverty in Maine 2010," prepared for the Maine Community Action Association, July 2010, http://www.mainecommunityaction.org.

18. David Vail, "Prospects for a Rim County Population Rebound: Can Quality of Place Lure In-Migrants?" *Maine Policy Review* (Winter/Spring 2010).

19. Acheson, "Poverty in Maine."

20. Ibid.

21. Maine County and State Population Projections, 2013–2028, State Planning Office, March 2010, http://www.maine.gov/spo/economics/.

22. "Milbridge Welcome Mat," editorial, *Bangor Daily News*, May 27, 2009.

23. Town of Milbridge minutes from "Public Hearing, USDA Project on Wyman Road," April 8, 2009.

24. From complaint filed in Hand in Hand/Mano en Mano, Inc. v. Town of Milbridge, Maine, and Michael Domrad, Eric Beal, George Brace, and Lewis Pinkham, filed in US District Court for the District of Maine, September 8, 2009; http://www.pacer.gov.

25. From "Memorandum for the United States as Amicus Curiae," filed by the US Department of Justice in Mano en Mano v. Milbridge, October 9, 2009, http://www.pacer.gov.

26. Sharon Kiley Mack, "Milbridge Upholds Building Moratorium," *Bangor Daily News*, September 29, 2009.

27. Craig Idlebrook, "Milbridge Workforce Housing Proposal Tangled Up in Lawsuits," *Working Waterfront*, February–March 2010.

28. From complaint filed in State of Maine v. Sherman Merchant and Benjamin Ray, Superior Court, August 17, 2010, documents provided to the author.

29. The injunction also prohibits violence for reasons of religion, sex, ancestry, national origin, physical or mental disability, or sexual orientation. A violation of the order is punishable by up to a year in jail and a $2,000 fine.

30. Sharon Kiley Mack, "Hand in Hand Apartments Open Doors in Milbridge," *Bangor Daily News*, June 27, 2011.

CHAPTER FOUR

1. The obliteration of the Napatree cottages was the subject of a musical,
Hurricane, written by Michael Holland and performed at the New
York Musical Theater Festival in 2009.

2. Gloria Russell, "Fire Districts to Face Scrutiny," *Westerly (RI) Sun*,
July 11, 2003.

3. "The Sea-Side—Summer Life at Watch Hill, RI," *New York Times*,
August 27, 1868.

4. Ardith M. Schneider and Roberta M. Burkhardt, *Watch Hill Then &
Now* (Westerly, RI: Watch Hill Preservation Society, 2005), 11.

5. Emily Dupuis, "Follow the Rules at Napatree . . . Or," *Westerly Sun*,
July 12, 2007.

6. Donita Taylor, "New Napatree Rules Spur Discussion," *Providence
Journal*, July 10, 2007.

7. According to Erin King, a wildlife biologist with the Rhode Island office of US Fish and Wildlife, when a threatened or endangered species
shows up on private land, it is the landowner's responsibility under
the Endangered Species Act to manage the species according to law.
Although they are under no obligation to do so, landowners may relieve themselves of that responsibility by partnering with Fish and
Wildlife. The piping plover was listed as a federally threatened species in 1986.

8. Dupuis, "Follow the Rules at Napatree."

9. Emily Dupuis, "Napatree's Dog-Gone Dispute," *Westerly Sun*, August 29, 2007.

10. Thomas W. Smith to Grant O. Simmons III, Chairman, Park Commission, June 22, 2007. After this letter, Smith subsequently outlined
his complaints in a humorous, five-page letter to Westerly's Town
Council, the town's rule-making authority. That bit of civic engage-
ment drew a behind-the-scenes censure from Chaplin Barnes, executive director of the Watch Hill Conservancy. In a February 9, 2008,
memo to the conservancy's board members (obtained by the author

via a Freedom of Information Act request), Barnes lamented Smith's decision to go "outside of Watch Hill and over the head of the District," calling it "extremely unfortunate."

11. Emily Dupuis, "Solicitor Clarifies Town Enforcement of Napatree Dog Laws," *Westerly Sun*, October 5, 2009.

12. Constitution of the State of Rhode Island and Providence Plantations, Article 1, Section 17, http://www.rilin.state.ri.us. The gathering of seaweed was a common practice by early farmers, who used it to fertilize their fields.

13. Paul M. Warner, "Carbon Beach Gates Open After Long Battle," *Canyon (CA) News*, June 5, 2005. Geffen eventually relented and agreed to open the gates during the day.

14. Richard Perez-Pena, "Along the Jersey Shore, a Struggle to Get to the Sand," *New York Times*, August 12, 2011.

15. Jackie Fitzpatrick, "Watch Hill Divided on Tourism," *Day* (New London, CT), July 25, 1984.

16. National Register of Historic Places Inventory-Nomination Form for Watch Hill Historic District, Continuation Sheet 58, http://www.preservation.ri.gov.

17. Minutes of Watch Hill Fire District Meeting, October 2007. Watch Hill did work with the town to institute architectural-design standards for the commercial area on Bay Street.

18. *American Aristocracy* was directed by Lloyd Ingraham and starred Douglas Fairbanks.

19. Megan Matteucci, "Postcard from the Edge: Fate of Landmark RI Hotel Hangs in Balance Over Zoning Issues," *Boston Globe*, August 8, 2004.

20. Steve Cartwright, "Aphrodite Revs Up Again," *Working Waterfront* (ME), March 2006. Through his real estate company and family foundation, Royce controls more than a dozen properties in Westerly's historic downtown. He has gradually acquired them with the stated intent of revitalization. Many people welcome his investment—especially his foundation's support for a new outdoor ice-skating rink downtown. Others are suspicious of his spreading reach and influence. (See Lisa Prevost, "Westerly, R.I., Waits for Its

Development Angel," *New York Times*, December 15, 2010.) Royce is also a partner in the recently restored Weekapaug Inn.

21. In 2010, in an unrelated matter, Girouard was sentenced to thirty months in federal prison for his role in a bribery scheme in Connecticut.

22. Westerly Land Records, Declaration of Restrictive Covenants, Book 1498, Page 3, recorded January 26, 2006.

23. David Brussat, "Ocean House Proudly Copies the Past," *Providence Journal*, May 20, 2010.

24. Lorraine Cademartori, "Charles Royce's Ocean House Resort Revival," *Forbes*, March 26, 2012, www.forbes.com.

25. Prevost, "Westerly, R.I., Waits for Its Development Angel."

26. Review of Seasons at the Ocean House, *Rhode Island Monthly*, September 2010.

27. The cove is part of a federal navigation project maintained by the US Army Corps of Engineers, New England District. A map of this project area can be found under "Projects" at http://www.nae.usace .army.mil/navigation.

28. "Obstructionist Shouldn't Deter Watch Hill Groups from Positive Programs," *Westerly Sun*, September 8, 2007.

29. Royce is not on the board of the conservancy, but he is a financial supporter. Most notably, in 2008, his family foundation awarded the organization $100,000, according to federal tax disclosures.

30. "Back to Life," *American Executive*, March 2011.

31. Minutes of Watch Hill Fire District Meeting, August 30, 2008.

32. Capt. Fred DeGrooth, "Proposed Closures on Napatree Point," *Westerly Sun*, July 13, 2011.

33. Grant Simmons III, chairman, Watch Hill Fire District Park Commission, to Randall Saunders, member, Westerly Harbor Commission, and attached draft of "proposed Watch Hill elements of the Westerly Harbor Management Plan," June 24, 2011.

34. Fred DeGrooth, author interview, August 2011, Westerly, RI.

35. Jane Buxton, "Napatree Point Conservation Area Ecosystem Management Study," Rhode Island Natural History Survey, July 2010, www.thewatchhillconservancy.org.

36. "Trespassing Lodged in Westerly Dispute," *Day*, September 17, 1977.

37. From decision in State v. James Ibbison III, 448 A.2d 728, Supreme Court of Rhode Island, July 20, 1982, http://www.scholar.google.com. The court's interpretation of the boundary between private property and public-trust lands was based on a much earlier US Supreme Court decision: Borax Consolidated Ltd. v. City of Los Angeles (1935).

38. Leslie Bowman, "Waterfront Property Rights Questioned in Coastal Dispute," *Working Waterfront*, September 28, 2011.

39. Carol Severance v. Jerry Patterson, March 30, 2012, decision by Supreme Court of Texas, http://www.supreme.courts.state.tx.us.

40. "Access to the Waterfront: Issues and Solutions Across the Nation," Maine Sea Grant College Program, University of Maine, http://www.seagrant.umaine.edu.

41. Elizabeth Williamson, "Just a Quiet Retreat, With a Few Rules," *Wall Street Journal*, August 28, 2010.

42. Geraldine Fabrikant, "Old Nantucket Warily Meets the New," *New York Times*, June 5, 2005. Nantucket authorities are trying to maintain the island's tradition of keeping beaches open to all by offering tax incentives and police patrols to landowners who agree to grant access to their sections of the sand. The initiative is called "One Big Beach."

43. Geraldine Baum, "Beach Policy Goes Against the Grain," *Los Angeles Times*, May 18, 2002.

44. "Designation of Public Rights-of-Way to the Tidal Areas of the State," Coastal Resource Management Council, Progress Reports for 2010–2011 and 2000–2001, http://www.crmc.ri.gov.

45. Decision in Rhode Island Mobile Sportfishermen v. Nope's Island Conservation Association, Rhode Island Superior Court, January 31, 2011, http://www.courts.ri.gov.

46. Tom Meade, "Hidden Nail Traps Planted on Disputed Road," *Providence Journal*, June 11, 2008.

47. Ibid.

48. Emily Dupuis, "Napatree Point Gate to Be Replaced," *Westerly Sun*, July 10, 2008.

49. "Guidelines for the Development of Municipal Harbor Management Plans," State of Rhode Island Coastal Resources Management Council, July 13, 2009, http://www.crmc.ri.gov.

50. "The Pawcatuck River Estuary and Little Narragansett Bay: An Interstate Management Plan," July 14, 1992, 140, http://www.crmc.ri.gov.

51. Joe Raho, Watch Hill Yacht Club Harbor Committee, to Watch Hill Harbor Mooring Members, April 1, 2010, Freedom of Information Act request. The letter reminded mooring holders of the rules, and notified them in bold type that, once a harbor-management plan is adopted, private rentals will not be allowed.

52. Grant Simmons III, chairman, Watch Hill Fire District Park Commission, and Chaplin Barnes, executive director, Watch Hill Conservancy, to James Steadman, chairman, Westerly Harbor Management Commission, May 24, 2012.

53. Don E. Morris, "Tired of Watching Public's Access to Shoreline Erode," letter to the editor, *Westerly Sun*, July 25, 2012.

54. Press release from the Rhode Island Office of the Attorney General, "Attorney General Kilmartin Files Lawsuit to Enforce Public's Right to Use Misquamicut Beach," September 18, 2012, http://www.riag.ri.gov.

CHAPTER FIVE

1. Harold L. Nash, *Historical Events on Noroton Neck* (Darien, CT: Darien Historical Society, 1974); "Thomas Crimmins, a Contractor, Dies," obituary, *New York Times*, December 19, 1968.

2. Darien Land Records, Book 77, 108–9. The easement was granted to Edwin D. Weed, a son of one of Darien's oldest and most prominent families.

3. James W. Loewen, *Sundown Towns: A Hidden Dimension of American Racism* (New York: Touchstone, 2005), 4.

4. Marcia Chambers, "Female Golfers Are Challenging Country Club Rules," *New York Times*, March 28, 1997.

5. Based on 2011 data compiled by William Raveis Real Estate, http://www.raveis.com.

6. The highest-priced property in Darien's history, a compound on Contentment Island, hit the market for $26 million in 2012.

7. Darien, CT: Assessor Database, http://darien.ias-clt.com/; John Davisson, "Property Sales: Top 25 from the First Half of 2011," *Darien (CT) Patch*, July 7, 2011.

8. From Christopher Stefanoni et al. v. Ian M. Duncan, Connecticut Appellate Court decision, November 1, 2005, http://www.jud.state.ct.us.

9. Connecticut General Statutes Section 8-30g. Also known as the Affordable Housing Land Use Appeals Act, http://www.cga.ct.gov.

10. Massachusetts General Laws (M.G.L.) Chapter 40B, §§ 20–23. Also known as the Comprehensive Permit Act, http://www.malegislature.gov.

11. In order to qualify for this appeals process, the project in question must set aside at least 30 percent of its units for households earning no more than 80 percent of either state or area median income, whichever is lower. The income requirements must be written into the deed and guaranteed to stay in place for at least forty years.

12. Terry J. Tondro, "Connecticut's Affordable Housing Appeals Statute: After Ten Years of Hope, Why Only Middling Results?" *Western New England Law Review* 23 (2001): 122.

13. As of 2010, according to the state Department of Economic and Community Development, 31 out of 169 Connecticut municipalities were exempt from 8-30g.

14. Eleanor Charles, "Darien's Rocky Road to Affordable Living," *New York Times*, February 14, 1993.

15. Lisa Prevost, "Resisting Affordable Homes in Darien," *New York Times*, November 13, 2005.

16. Ibid.

17. Ibid.

18. Vincent J. Moran, "DHS Removes 'Slave Auction' as Possible Party Theme," *Darien (CT) News-Review*, February 18, 2005.

19. Prevost, "Resisting Affordable Homes in Darien."

20. "Darien Land Trust Acquires 77 Nearwater Lane," press release, August 15, 2007, http://www.darienlandtrust.org.

21. Transcript of Mark Gregory's testimony before Ct. General Assembly Committee on Housing, February 2011, http://www.cga.ct.gov.

22. The film is based on the Broadway adaptation of Patrick Dennis's 1955 best-selling novel of the same name.

23. The film is based on Laura Z. Hobson's 1947 novel of the same name.

24. Robert M. Fogelson, *Bourgeois Nightmares: Suburbia, 1870–1930* (New Haven, CT: Yale University Press, 2005), 70–73.

25. *New York Times* classifieds, April 26, 1925.

26. James W. Loewen, *Lies Across America: What Our Historic Sites Get Wrong* (New York: New Press, 1999), 408.

27. David Anderson, "Darien Puts Curb on Church Camp," *New York Times*, June 15, 1955. The pastor for the church reported receiving harassing phone calls before finally deciding to drop the plan.

28. Richard H. Parkes, "Anti-Catholic Tracts Reported in Darien G.O.P. Headquarters," *New York Times*, September 23, 1960.

29. Gregory C. Coffin to Martin Luther King Jr., "Congratulations from Darien Public Schools Superintendent to MLK," January 4, 1965, Martin Luther King Jr. Center for Nonviolent Social Change, Atlanta, http://www.thekingcenter.org.

30. Martin Luther King Jr. to Gregory Coffin, "Draft Letter," undated, ibid.

31. William Borders, "Racial Barriers Scored in Darien; Departing Educator Fears Unrealism Among Youth of Affluent Community," *New York Times*, June 23, 1966.

32. "What Is Darien CT Like?" *UrbanBaby*, February 15, 2009, http://www.urbanbaby.com.

33. "Relocating to New York," chat room, *Mumsnet*, September 2004, http://www.mumsnet.com.

34. A more recent schools superintendent, Don Fiftal, raised some eyebrows a few years back when he declined to arrange for the in-school airing of President Obama's live message to students because, he said, it wasn't "compelling" enough to take away from academic time; Staff reports, "School Districts Take Different Approaches with Live Presidential Speech," *Stamford (CT) Advocate*, September 8, 2009.

35. The 2010 US Census data shows Darien with a black population of 0.5 percent. The proportion in surrounding suburbs is 0.99 percent

in New Canaan, 4.9 percent in Greenwich, and 1.2 percent in Westport and Fairfield. In Norwalk and Stamford, African Americans account for about 22 percent of the population. Darien's standing as the wealthiest town was reported by Siobhan Crise and John Davisson, "Nonprofit: Darien Wealthiest Town in Fairfield County," *Darien Patch*, May 20, 2011.

36. Robert M. Tomasson, "An Estate May Be Key to Breaking Darien's Ban on Apartments," *New York Times*, February 25, 1979.

37. Ibid.

38. Samuel G. Freedman, "A Town vs. a Region," *New York Times*, February 6, 1983. The consultant's warning of a potential exodus of executives drew scoffs from the director of a regional planning group, who pointed out that executives lived in every one of the area's towns, even those with a significant amount of multifamily housing.

39. Loewen, *Lies Across America*, 410.

40. Eleanor Charles, "Darien Voters Give Apartment Developer a Victory," *New York Times*, October 21, 2001.

41. Transcript of David Campbell's testimony before Ct. General Assembly Committee on Housing, February 2011, http://www.cga.ct.gov.

42. Interview on the Lisa Wexler radio show, October 12, 2008, http://lisawexler.com.

43. Builders don't necessarily like inclusionary zoning as it adds to their costs. In order to help subsidize the lower-priced units, inclusionary zoning ordinances often allow for slightly more units overall. Some ordinances, including Darien's, also give builders the option of paying a fee to the town for construction of affordable housing at another location.

44. "Fred Conze Considers Affordable Housing a Virus," YouTube video of a portion of the July 1, 2008, meeting of the Darien Planning and Zoning Commission.

45. The rule does not apply to single-family subdivisions with fewer than five building lots.

46. Austin Amoroso, "P&Z Hesitant to Change Zoning Laws Affordable Housing," *Darien (CT) Times*, June 5, 2008.

47. Lisa Prevost, "Who Should Get Affordable Homes?" *New York Times,* October 25, 2009.

48. In 2012, the Connecticut Fair Housing Center filed a federal lawsuit against the Winchester Housing Authority charging that it had taken residency preferences too far. The suit accuses the authority of only accepting Section 8 housing applications from people living in one of the seventeen northwestern Connecticut communities it serves. The African American plaintiff in the case claims she was turned away by the housing authority and advised to apply to housing programs in several Connecticut cities instead. Section 8 is the federal rental voucher program for low-income households.

49. Prevost, "Who Should Get Affordable Homes?"

50. Steven H. Rosenbaum, chief, Housing and Civil Enforcement Section, to First Selectman David Campbell, dated May 4, 2010.

51. Joshua Brustein, "Westchester Board Approves a Housing-Integration Pact," *New York Times,* September 23, 2009.

52. John Davisson, "P&Z Approves Priority Populations Change," *Darien Patch,* November 17, 2010.

53. "Data Interaction for Connecticut Mastery Test," Connecticut CMT and CAPT Online Reports website, http://www.ctreports.com; state Strategic School Profile 2009–10, Ct. State Department of Education, http://sdeportal.ct.gov.

54. For test scores: Connecticut CMT and CAPT Online Reports website; for demographic data: Connecticut Strategic School Profile 2009–10.

55. Ibid.

56. Jonathan Rothwell, "Housing Costs, Zoning, and Access to High-Scoring Schools" (Washington, DC: Metropolitan Policy Program at Brookings Institution, 2012).

57. Ibid., 21.

58. Frederick B. Conze, 2011 State of the Town address; http://www.darienct.gov.

59. Heather Schwartz, *Housing Policy Is School Policy: Economically Integrative Housing Promotes Academic Success in Montgomery County, Maryland* (New York: Century Foundation, 2010), 5, 33.

60. Darien Police reports, May 20, 2006, and August 21, 2006.

61. Memorandum of Decision, Christopher Stefanoni and Margaret Stefanoni v. Planning and Zoning Commission of Darien, Superior Court, Judicial District of New Britain, February 16, 2012.

62. During the fiscal year ending June 30, 2012, the town of Darien spent more than $300,000 on litigation with the Stefanonis. Susan Shultz, "Darien's Stefanoni Bills Top $300,000 for the Year," *Darien Times*, June 21, 2012.

63. Town of Darien Affordable Housing Plan, approved August 24, 2009, 4, http://www.darienct.gov.

64. E-mail from Dave Campbell to selectmen, February 24, 2010. This e-mail was first revealed by the *Darien News* in an article reported by Maggie Gordon: "Stefanonis: Town Does Not Qualify for Moratorium," June 10, 2010.

65. All thirty Clock Hill homes are restricted to moderate-income households, which are defined at length in the deed restrictions as households "that have gross family income at or below seventy percent of the then-current Connecticut Housing Finance Authority (CHFA) income guidelines by family size, which are promulgated on a county basis and adjusted annually by CHFA, in any event not to exceed 115% of the median income for the area, as determined by . . . [HUD]." Recorded at volume 776, page 513, of the Darien Land Records.

66. Lisa Prevost, "A Fair-Housing Inquiry in Darien," *New York Times*, October 8, 2010.

67. The state's interpretation of the deed restriction (explained in note 64) is that it defines the income limit as 70 percent of 115 percent of area median income. This interpretation ignores the reference to the Connecticut Housing Finance Authority income guidelines. But 70 percent of 115 percent works out to 80.5 percent of area median income—still more than 80 percent but close enough, in the state's opinion.

68. John D. Hertz, Darien town counsel, to A. Vincent Falconi, executive director, Darien Housing Authority, August 8, 1997. Memo attached

from John Madeo, president, Fairfield 2000 Homes Corp., to Charles E. Janson, Esq., August 7, 1997. Darien Housing Authority, www .darienct.gov.

69. E-mail from Jenny Schwartz, chairman, Darien Housing Authority, to commission members, November 1, 2010, FOIA request.

70. John Wayne Fox to Commissioner Joan McDonald, November 12, 2010, Connecticut Department of Economic and Community Development.

71. Ibid.

72. E-mail from Timothy Hollister to Jeremy Ginsberg, Wayne Fox, and Michael Santoro, November 17, 2010, FOIA request.

73. E-mail from Kathryn Molgano, executive director, Darien Housing Authority, to Jennifer Schwartz, board chair, Darien Housing Authority, October 22, 2010, FOIA request.

74. Letter from Timothy Hollister to Commissioner Joan MacDonald, December 28, 2010, provided to the author by Hollister.

75. Letter from Joan McDonald, economic development commissioner, to Greenwich first selectman Peter Tesei, July 15, 2010, FOIA request to Department of Economic and Community Development (DECD). The terms of the housing-for-land agreement were spelled out in a 1987 state law: The state would give Greenwich a thirteen-acre site containing a mothballed power plant at the mouth of the Mianus River. Greenwich could use up to 75 percent of the power-plant land for recreational purposes. The remaining land was to be reserved for low- to moderate-income housing. In 1997, Greenwich officials had the deal amended to allow them to put the housing elsewhere in town—but they never did. In 2010, the town's argument to Commissioner McDonald was that Greenwich had effectively met its obligation by allotting some of its federal Community Development Block Grant funds to help support a few privately developed housing projects in town. But no town land or town resources were ever provided.

76. Memorandum to Commissioner Joan McDonald from Jonathan Du-Bois, chairman, Greenwich Housing Authority, and Anthony Johnson, executive director, September 2, 2010, FOIA request.

77. Phone interview with John Wayne Fox, January 3, 2011.

78. Memorandum of Decision in Christopher Stefanoni, et al. v. Department of Economic Community Development and Town of Darien, Connecticut Superior Court, Judicial District of New Britain, June 19, 2012.

79. Christopher Hamer et al. v. Darien Planning and Zoning Commission and Frederick B. Conze, US District Court of Connecticut, November 28, 2011.

80. Susan Shultz, "New Lawsuit Accuses Darien's P&Z Commission of Anti-African-American Agenda," *Darien Times*, December 3, 2011.

81. Susan Shultz, "Department of Justice Closes Case on Darien, Two Years Later," *Darien Times*, August 31, 2012.

CHAPTER SIX

1. Some argue that the state's business-enterprise tax, a tax based on the wages businesses pay, is essentially a broad-based tax.

2. Ryan Forster and Kail Padgitt, "Where Do State and Local Governments Get Their Tax Revenue?" Fiscal Fact No. 242, Tax Foundation, August 27, 2010, http://taxfoundation.org. As of 2011, New Hampshire ranked last in the nation for state support for higher education per $1,000 of personal income; "State Fiscal Support for Higher Education FY1961 to FY2011," *Postsecondary Education Opportunity* (Oskaloosa, IA) 224 (February 2011): 1-20, http://www.postsecondary.org.

3. As of the 2010 US Census, New Hampshire's population had a median age of 41.1, the fourth highest in the nation.

4. For deeper insight into traditional New Hampshire culture, check out the well-known list of "100 Things You Should Do To Know the Real New Hampshire," compiled by Steve Taylor, a longtime state agriculture commissioner, journalist, and farmer; http://www.leadershipnh.org.

5. C. Christine Fillmore, "Home Rule: Do New Hampshire Towns Have It?" New Hampshire Local Government Center, February 2010, http://www.nhlgc.org.

6. "Ossipee, NH," Economic and Labor Market Information Bureau, New Hampshire Employment Security, http://www.nhes.nh.gov.

7. Ossipee Master Plan, chapter 3: "Land Use," http://www.ossipee.org.

8. The federal Low Income Housing Tax Credit (LIHTC) program provides an indirect subsidy to finance development of affordable rental housing. The tax credits are designated to state agencies, which then award the credits to developers on a competitive basis. Developers sell the credits to investors to raise equity they would otherwise have to borrow. Eligibility is restricted to projects in which at least 40 percent of the rentals are available only to households with incomes below 60 percent of the area median income, or alternatively, at least 20 percent of the units are reserved for households earning no more than 50 percent of the area median income.

9. Russ Thibeault, "Ossipee Housing Needs Assessment," September 14, 2004. Prepared at the request of Great Bridge Properties in conjunction with litigation in Great Bridge Properties, LLC v. Town of Ossipee. Copy provided to author by William Caselden.

10. Ossipee Master Plan, chapter 6: "Economic Base Update," http://www.ossipee.org.

11. "Ossipee, NH," Economic and Labor Market Information Bureau, New Hampshire Employment Security, http://www.nhes.nh.gov.

12. Joie Finley Morris, homeless outreach worker, Tri-County Community Action Program, author interview July 8, 2011.

13. Marge Webster, Tri-County Community Action Program, recorded comments from public hearing on Great Bridge application before Ossipee Zoning Board of Adjustment, December 10, 2002. Tapes provided to author by Bill Caselden.

14. Brian W. Blaesser et al., "Advocating Affordable Housing in New Hampshire: The Amicus Curiae Brief of the American Planning Association in *Wayne Britton v. Town of Chester,*" *Journal of Urban and Contemporary Law* (Washington University) 40, no. 3 (1991): 10, http://digitalcommons.law.wustl.edu.

15. Warren Hastings, "Chester Zoning Decision Called a Win for Poor," *Union Leader* (NH), July 26, 1991.

16. Wayne Britton v. Town of Chester, 134 N.H. 434, 595 A.2d 492 (1991), http://scholar.google.com.

17. The language is roughly based on a model developed by the federal government in the 1920s called the Standard State Zoning Enabling Act.

18. The statute granting towns zoning authority is NH RSA 674:16.

19. Kirstin Downey, "Ruling May Encourage Multifamily Housing; New Hampshire Zoning Case Called Landmark," *Washington Post*, August 24, 1991.

20. The 1975 New Jersey case was Southern Burlington County NAACP v. Township of Mount Laurel. The New Jersey supreme court held that the township's zoning ordinance violated the general welfare provision of its state constitution by not providing a real opportunity for construction of its "fair share" of the regional need for low- and moderate-income housing. Eight years later, in *Mt. Laurel II*, the court revisited the case and ruled that when municipalities had failed to meet their obligation, lower courts could step in and overturn local zoning regulations to allow housing projects to go forward.

21. Downey, "Ruling May Encourage Multifamily Housing."

22. Hastings, "Chester Zoning Decision."

23. Downey, "Ruling May Encourage Multifamily Housing."

24. Town of Chester, NH Master Plan, adopted November 1, 2006, 46, http://www.chesternh.org.

25. Ibid., 138.

26. These homes are located in three different subdivisions that were developed under an earlier cluster-housing ordinance that granted density bonuses to developers if they designated at least 20 percent of the units as affordable.

27. Cynthia Roberts, Chester planning coordinator, author interview March 21, 2012. The open space subdivision allows housing to be clustered on smaller lots than usual provided that at least 50 percent of the site is deed-restricted as conservation land. The ordinance allows for a density bonus of 25 percent more units to developers who include some workforce housing, but no more than half of all the housing in the subdivision may be multifamily. So far, Roberts says, the ordinance has only been used for market-rate, single-family homes.

28. Harry Merrow, author interview, Ossipee Town Hall, July 5, 2011.

29. Great Bridge Properties' Motion for Rehearing before Ossipee Zoning Board of Adjustment, January 7, 2003. Copy provided to author by Bill Caselden.

30. New Hampshire has a statute that directs municipalities on how to assess multifamily rental properties developed under the Low Income Housing Tax Credit program.

31. Taped recording of public hearing before Ossipee Zoning Board of Adjustment, December 10, 2002. Tape provided to author by Bill Caselden.

32. Ibid.

33. Great Bridge Properties, LLC v. Town of Ossipee, "Findings, Rulings and Orders," Strafford County Superior Court, February 7, 2005, http://www.courts.state.nh.us.

34. Elisabeth Wisner, "The Puritan Background of the New England Poor Laws," *Social Service Review* 19 (1945): 1.

35. Edward M. Cook Jr., *Ossipee New Hampshire 1785–1985: A History* (Portsmouth, NH: Peter E. Randall Publisher, 1989).

36. Ibid.

37. The municipal welfare statute is NH RSA 165: Aid to Assisted Persons.

38. Keith E. Bates, "Local Welfare Budgets Hit Hard by State and National Economic Conditions," *New Hampshire Town and City*, November/December 2009; Joe Magruder, "NH Senate Sticks with May 30 Memorial Day," Associated Press, April 12, 1985.

39. Under the statute, a welfare office providing assistance to a person with a residence elsewhere can seek reimbursement from that town.

40. Nate Giarnese, "Ossipee Keeping Eye Out for Welfare Abusers," *Conway (NH) Daily Sun*, April 3, 2006.

41. Ossipee Master Plan, chapter 6: "Economic Base Update."

42. "Carroll County Commuting Patterns," Economic and Labor Market Information Bureau, NH Employment Security, 2000, http://www.nhes.nh.gov.

43. William Ray, "Deconstructing the Myths: Housing Development versus School Costs," *Communities & Banking*, Federal Reserve Bank of Boston, Spring 2005, http://www.bos.frb.org.

44. Peter Francese, "Age-Restricted Housing in New England," *Communities & Banking*, Federal Reserve Bank of Boston, Fall 2008, http://www.bos.frb.org.

45. Russ Thibeault, "Housing and School Enrollment in New Hampshire: An Expanded View," prepared for New Hampshire Housing Finance Authority, May 2005, http://www.nhhfa.org.

46. Dr. Lisa K. Shapiro, "Housing New Hampshire's Workforce," prepared for the New Hampshire Workforce Housing Council (2005): 2, http://www.workforcehousingnh.com.

47. "New Hampshire Fall Enrollments 1974 to 2005," NH Office of Energy and Planning. Russ Thibeault, "Who Lives in NH Housing?," Demographic and School Enrollment Trends, Phase 1 Report, (2011), prepared for NH Housing Finance Authority, http://www.nhhfa.org.

48. Francese, "Age-Restricted Housing in New England."

49. Peter Francese and Lorraine Stuart Merrill, *Communities & Consequences: The Unbalancing of New Hampshire's Human Ecology, & What We Can Do About It* (Portsmouth, NH: Peter E. Randall Publishers, 2008).

50. Ibid., 5–6.

51. Kenneth M. Johnson, "New Hampshire Demographic Trends in the Twenty-First Century," Reports on New England No. 4, Carsey Institute, University of New Hampshire, 2012, 13, http://www.carseyinstitute.unh.edu. Johnson notes that, in 2010, 13.5 percent of New Hampshire's population was sixty-five or older, a level very close to the national average.

52. Ibid., 11.

53. Francese also believes that school districts are far too numerous in New England, due to the cultural allegiance to local control. He frequently points out that New England has ten to twenty school districts per county, compared to the one or two per county in the more populous state of Florida.

54. Steve Norton, "New Hampshire's Silver Tsunami: Aging and the Health Care System," NH Center for Public Policy Studies (2011): 1, http://www.nhpolicy.org.

55. Ibid., 10–11.

56. During the case, McConkey testified in court that he opposed the project and would vote against it again. But that may have just been politics. McConkey now lives one town over, in Freedom, and in an interview in 2011, he told me that he had thought the project's location was appropriate and had been "absolutely amazed" by the opposition. He also said that he'd made his public comments about the ordinance's exclusionary intent knowing full well that what he'd said was "enough to let the appeal process go forward"; author interview.

57. Great Bridge Properties, LLC v. Town of Ossipee.

58. Bill Caselden, author interview, March 21, 2011.

59. RSA 674:58–61. The law defines workforce housing as (a) for-sale housing affordable for people earning up to 100 percent of area median income and (b) multifamily rentals affordable for tenants making no more than 60 percent of area median income for a three-person household.

60. The legislation was House Bill 368-FN-LOCAL, "An Act relative to workforce housing and the definition of community," 2011 Session of the NH General Court, http://www.gencourt.state.nh.us.

CONCLUSION

1. Crystal Carter and the Connecticut Fair Housing Center v. Housing Authority of the Town of Winchester, US District Court for the District of Connecticut, August 1, 2012, http://www.pacer.gov.

2. Carol Morello, "Study: Rich, Poor Americans Increasingly Likely to Live in Separate Neighborhoods," *Washington Post*, August 1, 2012.

3. Ibid.

4. Peter Applebome, "Despite 2009 Deal, Affordable Housing Roils Westchester," *New York Times*, April 3, 2012.

5. Paul McMorrow, "Hingham Standoff Shows Pitfalls of State's Affordable Housing Law," *Boston Globe*, July 10, 2012.

6. S. Mitra Kalita and Robbie Whelan, "No McMansions for Millennials," *Developments* blog, *Wall Street Journal*, January 13, 2011.

7. Brad Broberg, "Housing for the Generations," *On Common Ground*, National Association of Realtors, Summer 2012.

8. Roger Showley, "U.S. Overbuilt in Big Houses, Planners Find," *San Diego Union-Tribune*, February 2, 2012.

9. Broberg, "Housing for the Generations."

10. Christopher B. Leinberger, "Now Coveted: A Walkable, Convenient Place," *New York Times*, May 25, 2012.

INDEX

A Better Chance program, 104, 111
affordable housing: belief that affordable housing hurts neighborhoods, 55, 160n15; *Britton v. Chester* and, 128–30, 138–39, 141; demographic consequences of limited availability, 36–37; demographic shifts that could refocus housing developments, 146–48; economics of smaller houses and lots, 27; housing discrimination lawsuit against Winchester, 143–44; *Mt. Laurel* decision and, 129, 175n20; neighborhoods' increasing segregation by income, 144; restrictive zoning's impact on students, 145–46; Section 8-30g law and, 97–98, 112, 114–19, 167n11, 167n13; typical local response to housing proposals, 54–55. *See also* Chapter 40B; Darien, Connecticut; Easton, Massachusetts; exclusionary zoning;

Milbridge, Maine; Ossipee, New Hampshire
Affordable Housing Land Use Appeals Act. *See* Section 8-30g law
Altomare, Kim, 140–41
American Apartheid (Massey and Denton), 33
American Aristocracy (film), 77, 163n18
Ames family (Easton, Massachusetts), 26, 41
"Aryan from Darien," 101–3
Auntie Mame (film), 101
Austin, Candace, 63
AvalonBay Communities, 104

baby boomers, 17, 137, 146–47
Barnes, Chaplin B., 72, 73, 82, 83, 84, 91, 162n10
Beacon Communities, 41
Beddard, Michael, 79
Bentley, April, 65
Bernhardt Meadows (Roxbury, Connecticut), 14
Berry, Elliott, 128, 141, 142